Faith: The Gift of God

FAITH:
The Gift of God

TOM WELLS

THE BANNER OF TRUTH TRUST

THE BANNER OF TRUTH TRUST
3 Murrayfield Road, Edinburgh EH12 6EL
PO Box 621, Carlisle, Pennsylvania 17013, USA

*

© Tom Wells 1983
First published 1983
ISBN 0 85151 361 1

*

Set in 11 on 12 pt VIP Plantin
Filmset, printed and bound in Great Britain by
Hazell Watson & Viney Ltd, Aylesbury, Bucks

Contents

A Word of Introduction

The road of life turns in queer and unexpected directions. Take the fact that you and I are meeting in the pages of this book over a subject that would not have interested us in the least at one time. That is an odd turn. Perhaps there was a day when we ridiculed 'faith', jeering at and mocking those who were devoted to 'religion' as men call it. Or – more probably, for this is so common in our age – we were indifferent to faith. We were content to be without it in a world that demands tangible things, silver and gold, bus tokens and airline tickets.

'Faith won't get you far in *this* world,' we may have said. If the remark did not strike us as profound we felt it was safe. Who could argue with it? Really *argue*, I mean, with 'hard facts' to back them up – who indeed?

Then the road took an unexpected turn. Perhaps we thought life was leading us to wealth, to material success, but it went the other way. Maybe it was the security of rich and stimulating friendships that we expected around the turn. But we found boredom and loneliness. Around this bend in life's road dark shadows fell across our path. Now we groped for the things we had formerly plunged headlong after. We reached out, cautiously felt for them, but they were gone. In fact, they had never been there, for us, at all.

'Vanity, vanity, all is vanity,' we may have cried, borrowing the words of the writer of Ecclesiastes. Many have come to Christ on a path such as this.

Perhaps your road turned another way. Maybe the curve your life made brought you the very things you sought. Heady with success, you thought that all was well. 'Eat, drink, and be merry!' was your motto. The words are old, but the sentiment is very much with us. Yet the very abundance of 'satisfying' things gradually brought dissatisfaction. The streams of earth, that promised to quench your thirst when you saw them far off, turned insipid. You discovered this truth: 'A man's life does not consist in the abundance of *things* that he possesses.' Many have come to Christ by this path also.

Perhaps your road was stranger yet. Suddenly life turned a corner that brought you face-to-face with Jesus Christ. You can give no account of it at all. One day He was not in sight; the next He filled your view. Your life reminds us of that word of God: 'I was found of them who sought me not.' Not a few have come to Christ on this path as well.

Someone has said: 'There are many ways to Christ, but only one way to God.' That is true. Our histories before we met Christ are as varied as our tastes or the shapes of our noses. Yet each of us who has come to God has come by Christ. 'I am the way,' He said. 'No one comes to the Father except by me' (John 14:6). No one? 'No one!' 'For without me, you can do nothing' (John 15:5). Later on He moved one of His followers to declare: 'Neither is there salvation in any other: for there is none other name under heaven given among men, whereby we must be saved' (Acts 4:12). Many ways to Christ, but one way to God!

In the brief sketches above I have described the

journey of some of us until the hour when Jesus Christ appeared in our paths. This book is about *what happened then*. Imagine the scene once more. Routinely plodding along, you lift your eyes. Startled, you gaze at Him. Who is this? What will you do with Him? Will you repel Him? No! you embrace Him. That is the way it was.

You embrace Him? This moment needs some explanation.

This little book is a book of *theology*. We must not let that word scare us. Theology is simply the study of God and His relations to the things He has made. So much theology seems to be locked up in forbidding-looking volumes with five-syllable words. How sad! This book, however, is an attempt to write theology for the ordinary man, for people like you and me. More specifically, it is about the theology of salvation. It is about the part God played in our coming to Christ. There are few subjects more important than this, as every Christian knows.

If this volume should fall into the hands of someone who does not yet see the importance of God's salvation, that would also make me happy. If you are such a person, please stay with me. If I have earlier failed to sketch your life because you have not come to Christ there is truth for *you* in these pages. Let us set out, together.

1: *Making a Start*

When I approach a question, any question, there are two things I need to do to make a start. First, I must define my question. That is, I must be quite sure what it is I want to know. All fuzziness must go. If my question is not clear in my mind I shall make many false starts. Who can tell where I will end up?

One other thing is necessary. I must know where to turn for my answer. When I have these two things, a sharply defined question and a place to find the answer, I am on my way to learning. This way of 'finding out' is so much a part of me that I may not notice that I use it constantly. But I do.

I suppose I started this process when I was a child. Back then my questions were simple and often sharply defined. For instance, 'Where's my mummy?' Or, 'When do we eat?' How nice it would be if all the questions I face today were equally clear! Because my world was small I had only one place, at first, to get my answers. From my parents!

As I grew, my horizons expanded. Questions became more complex. Sources for answers multiplied. Now I have to labour to simplify my questions. Now I have to sort out the possible places to find my answers.

In this chapter I want you to look over my shoulder. No, I want more than that, I want you to join me in this process. My question will be: 'Is faith a gift of

God?' But what does that mean, and what does it not mean? We'll have to define it further. If I am talking about one thing, and you have something else in mind, we are not likely to get far together.

And where shall we find the answer? You have already decided that question, as I also have. In the Bible! But why the Bible? Are there no other sources equally good? We'll look into that in this chapter as well.

What do I mean when I ask, 'Is faith the gift of God?' Go back with me to the point where I left you in my introduction. You are travelling the path we call 'life'. Perhaps the pace is brisk, perhaps sluggish. All at once you come upon Jesus Christ. Who is this? What will you do with Him? Others have asked Him to step aside, to be gone. Will you? No! Instead you embrace Him. 'This moment,' I wrote, 'needs some explanation.'

When I said you 'embraced' Christ I called on a picture. I meant, of course, that you trusted in Jesus Christ as Saviour and Lord – as *your* Saviour and *your* Lord. You turned to Him for forgiveness and for help against yourself, against your sins. You put your faith in Jesus Christ. That is what men do when they become Christians. That is what you did.

Now the question is: why did you do this? Why did you turn to Christ? You know well that others have turned away from Him. Still, you did not. You put your faith in Him. When I ask, 'Is faith the gift of God?', I am looking at your faith. I am not speaking of the mere capacity to believe which we all share. Belief in this thing or that person is very much a part of daily life. But I am looking at the kind of faith in which a man turns from his sin to trust in the Lord Jesus Christ. Is that kind of faith the gift of God?

Let me sharpen my question further. If Mr. Jones puts his faith in Jesus Christ, has God given Mr. Jones something to move Mr. Jones to believe – something that God has withheld from Mr. Smith who remains an unbeliever? Who makes the difference here? Does Jones (or Smith) make the difference? Or does God?

If you now grasp my question you also see why we will need a book to discuss it. Very different answers have been given to this question. By Christians. By true believers. Yet the question is an important one. Why? Because it bears on our whole understanding of salvation. And that is not all. It bears heavily on the grandest subject of all – the character of God. May God grant us together a richer understanding of His person and His great salvation!

Earlier I told you that this is a book of theology. 'Theology', I said, 'is simply the study of God and His relations to the things He has made.' I encouraged you not to fear the word 'theology'. In one sense, in fact, every study is a study of theology at bottom. Every question is a theological question in a way. The question 'Where's my mummy?' does not look theological. But it certainly touches theology. If God had created nothing, not even mummies, the answer would have to be, 'Nowhere!' Leave God out and no question will be meaningful. And – there will be no one to ask a question!

Let me pursue this a bit further. Suppose we want to ask a question about nature. Let's say our question is, 'What is my relation to the grass and the trees?' This is an *ecological* question. Ecology is the study of man's relation to his environment. We hear a great deal about ecology today. Men are becoming more concerned about the effects of their actions on their environment. That environment includes the grass and the trees. This, however, is a theological question too. If we know what the Bible says – that men and grass and trees are creations of God – we will answer our question differently than if we deny that fact. So, you see, we are only a hair's breadth away from theology when we ask *any* question.

But questions differ. Some may start in theology and soon turn in other directions. Others are largely theological throughout. For instance, if we keep in mind God's creatorship we can turn from the Bible and go on to look at the book of nature in answering the question, 'What is my relation to the grass and the trees?' We may find an abundance of satisfaction in studying the grass and trees themselves. And an abundance of knowledge.

Our question, however, is of the other kind. With the question, 'Is faith the gift of God?' we do not find our basic principle in the Word of God and then turn to study man apart from the Scriptures. Let us be clear about this. This is the kind of question that depends *directly* on God's giving us the information. If the Word of God is silent we must be silent. If it speaks we can do nothing else but listen.

If I seem to be labouring this point, forgive me. I have good reason. My experience shows that this question does not always get a fair, biblical treatment. Quite often, it seems, Christians want to call in what they call 'common sense' to answer this question. I hope I am not opposed to common sense. That would be serious indeed. But we have the Scriptures just because common sense is inadequate here, at the point where man meets his Maker. I do not oppose common sense, which I suppose means 'good judgment'. Judgment, however, must be exercised on facts. The facts, in this case, are in the Word of God. To the Word of God we must go. There we must stay.

We have made a start by defining our question and by finding a place to get an answer. Our question is: 'Is faith – that faith which turns to and embraces Christ – the gift of God?' The Bible has the answer. We hope to find it together. There is one more thing to do in making a good start, however. To find it let us return to Mr. Smith and Mr. Jones.

Jones trusts in Christ. Smith does not. How often we see this situation. Two men hear the gospel. As far as we can tell, one is as likely to receive Christ as the other. They come from similar backgrounds. Their temperaments are alike. Their susceptibility to influence seems the same. Yet one makes a decided turnabout and the other does not. One turns in faith to Christ; the other turns away. In other matters both exercise faith in many of the same people and things each day. But at this point they go their separate ways. What is different about *this* act of faith? What does Jones have that Smith lacks?

The obvious answer to the question 'What does Jones have that Smith lacks?' is, in a word, *inclination*. Or, to use a simpler word, *desire*. Jones *desires* Christ; Smith does not. Jones is *inclined* to turn to Christ; Smith is not. That is the obvious answer, and it is the right one. But where does it take us? Not far, surely!

Not far, but far enough. The thing in which Mr. Jones differs from Mr. Smith is in his desire. Knowing this gets us into the Scriptures, because they have a good deal to say about men's desires. It helps us frame the question, 'What kind of a man desires Christ?' Or, 'What kind of man is inclined to turn to God?' The rest of this chapter will take up that question.

I mentioned common sense above. Before we turn to the Scriptures let us pause to see what common sense says. What kind of a man desires to turn to God? Common sense says, 'A wise man!' No one could argue with that, could he? Surely it is not the foolish man who turns to Christ, but the wise man. This logic seems ironclad. Maybe old Mr. Common Sense is not so stupid after all!

But just here I feel a difficulty. You will feel it too, I think, if I make it a bit more personal. It is this. It is all well and good to talk about some man somewhere turning to Christ because he is wise. But my conscience – not to mention the Bible – will not let me apply this solution to myself. Why did *I* desire Christ? If I answer, 'Because I was wise', my own heart rises up in protest. It seems very logical. But every Christian instinctively turns away from this solution when it is applied to himself, doesn't he? You had a friend, perhaps, who heard the gospel about the same time you did, yet he rejected it. He did not want it. Why did you receive it? Because you were a wise man or woman, and that's that? I think I hear you saying, 'No, I'm not your man. Whatever it was, it was not my wisdom that brought me to Christ!'

We must turn to God's Word for the answer to the question: 'What kind of a man desires to turn to God?' 'What kind of a man is inclined to turn to Christ?'

Now, right off, we run into a puzzle. I can get at it

best by quoting two things the Scriptures say. Of Christ they say, 'There is no beauty that we should desire him' (Isaiah 53:2). Of God they declare, 'There is none that seeketh after God' (Romans 3:11). The puzzle is this. We are quite sure that we see men who desire Christ, who seek after God. Yet the Scripture seems to deny that there are any such men or women or boys or girls at all. And, as if that were not bad enough, this same Bible goes on to command men to do these very things. Here is a riddle indeed!

How shall we find our way out of this maze? Well, that is what this book is about. Let me tell you first what I think we must not do. We must not pare down Scripture. I fear we sometimes do that. We do not let the Scriptures speak their mind, God's mind. But neither must we throw up our hands in despair. We must not say, 'It's all beyond me, I give up.' No, God gave us His Word to teach us. We must sit down before it as little children. We must pray God that it will instruct us.

The Bible's view of human nature is not a pretty one. Most Christians realize this. It is not hidden away in some obscure chapter of a little-known Old Testament book. No, it is right there on the surface of the Scriptures. Men are sinners, rebels; yes, even haters of God. In fact, if we take the Bible at all seriously, we see that human nature is a far more hellish thing than we could have guessed without the Bible's help.

It is possible to misunderstand this, of course. God made man in His own image. In some sense that image remains. We do not want to deny that. But the image is badly marred. Man is not like a bronze image of some great person that has been melted down to mere metal once more. Man has not lost all his likeness to

God. He is rather like a statue that has been ravaged by vandals and blighted by the elements until the likeness is largely disfigured. Or we can change the comparison. Man is spoiled, not as some children are spoiled, but as food is spoiled. This is man as God sees him. One way to put this, as I put it above, is to call man *a hater of God*. Let us see if we can get hold of what this means.

I think I must start by making good my charge that man is a hater of God. Earlier I did not stop to prove from the Bible that men are evil. I said that it lies on the surface of the Scriptures for all to see. And so it does. But when I put it in these terms – hating God – it may seem so extreme to some that they cannot, with the best will, suppose that I am right. I do not blame them. At one time I would have had the same hesitation. Yet the point must be made. I might almost say that, without getting this point, you will certainly miss the heart of what we mean by 'the grace of God'. Our experience of His grace is the grand thing that it is to us, just because we first received it when we – you and I – were haters of God.

We will let the Lord Jesus tell us about man's attitude towards God. On the night He was betrayed Jesus said:

If the world hate you, ye know that it hated me before it hated you. If ye were of the world, the world would love his own: but because ye are not of the world, but I have chosen you out of the world, therefore the world hateth you. Remember the word that I said unto you, The servant is not greater than his lord. If they have persecuted me, they will also persecute you; if they have kept my saying, they will keep yours also. But all these things will they do unto you for my name's sake, because they know not him that sent me. If I had not come and spoken unto them, they had not had sin: but now they have no cloke for their sin. He that hateth me hateth my Father also. If I had not done among them the works which none other man did, they had not had sin: but now have they both seen and hated both me and my Father (John 15:18–24).

What did Jesus mean by these words? They contain three main ideas:

1. Jesus' followers must expect hatred from the world (vv. 18–21)
2. The world's hatred is hatred of Christ also (vv. 20–24)
3. The world's hatred of Christ is hatred of His Father as well (vv. 23, 24).

So the world hates God. But what is this 'world' that hates God and Christ? And what does it have to do with you and me? It is the world of unconverted men. These men – and remember, we were such men – have something and someone other than Christ as King. 'We will not have this man to rule over us' is their motto. Every man must have a master, a king, over him. So the Bible sometimes pictures man as being under a thing – sin – as king. Sometimes it views man as under a person – Satan – as king. The choice is: sin and Satan, or God. A man loves God, and hates sin and Satan. Or he loves sin and Satan, and hates God. There is no middle ground. There was none for us when we were unconverted. We were part of the 'world'. We were on *that* side of the fence. We were haters of God. The Scriptures make that plain.

If you still hesitate to think of men as haters of God, perhaps a further word will help. It may be that you find yourself at a loss to square what God's Word teaches with your own past life. 'It simply comes to this,' you may say, 'I don't remember hating God at all.'

I think I know what you mean. As I look back at my own life I cannot call to mind an instance of feeling a dislike for God. Mind you, I do not say I never did dislike God. We all know how partial our memories may be. But, if I did, I cannot recall it. Disliking God, however, and hating Him are not the same thing. There is a difference here worth lingering over.

Just now there comes to mind something that may help me spell out what I mean. We have all heard two men talking about a third fellow, who is not present, in some such terms as these: 'Oh, I love John all right – I just don't like him!' Does that sound impossible to do? Maybe a bit of hypocrisy? No doubt it often is. But it need not be. Somewhere C. S. Lewis tells us how he changed his mind on this matter. One day he realized that this was the very way he often felt towards himself. He kept on *loving* C. S. Lewis, but there were times when he could not *like* himself at all! Most of us could say the same about ourselves, couldn't we? Loving and liking, then, must not be the same thing. Neither must hating and disliking.

From the Bible's point of view we love someone when we seek his benefit, when we seek to do him good. Think, for example, of the Good Samaritan. According to the Scriptures he loved his neighbour. The Samaritan loved his neighbour by seeking to save his life when he found the man lying helpless and half dead at the side of the road (Luke 10:25–37). The story tells us something of the Samaritan's feelings – he felt compassion. But it does not stop to ask whether he *liked* the half-dead man. Imagine yourself as the Samaritan. Would you have liked the man you helped?

Isn't the answer just this: you would not have known enough about him to like him or dislike him? Feelings of revulsion, akin to dislike, might have arisen at the sight of his souring wounds. You would have overcome those feelings. You would have loved him and helped him. You would have done it, however, without liking him.

It was said of the early Christians that they loved one another before they ever met. Could it have been said that they liked one another without meeting? Surely not! Liking or disliking cannot be done in advance. I can plan to love and help a man I have never met. But I can only hope (and pray) that I will like him.

The reverse is also true. You can find this same sort of contrast in the ideas of hate and dislike. It applies to men's attitudes towards God. If you went around your block and took a survey, asking the question 'Do you hate God?', I am pretty sure we both know what you would find. Your neighbours would lift their hands in horror. 'Hate God!' they would cry. 'Not me!' Hardly anyone would admit to so gross a crime.

I fear, though, that they would really be answering another question. You would use the word 'hate', but they would hear the word 'dislike'. They would be answering the question, 'Do you dislike God?' Except for an odd person here and there who has come to think of God as a cosmic spoilsport, the gist of their answers would be this: 'Why should I dislike Him? He's never done anything to me.' And you might well believe them. You have to be in touch with someone to like him or dislike him!

But hating is something else. Jesus was talking about it when He said, 'He that is not with me is against me'

(Luke 11:23). That is a remarkable statement. It is just the sort of statement that the man of the world finds impossible to accept. But it is true. It might be put this way: he that does not love Jesus hates Him. The Lord recognizes no middle ground. Just the place that the average man would like to stand on Jesus takes away. 'One side or the other,' He says.

If love is seeking someone's benefit, aiming to help someone, it might seem that hate would be seeking someone's harm, aiming to injure him. In that case there would be a third option, to do neither. But that is not the way God sees it. In God's view hatred is failing to seek the other person's benefit, failing to aim at helping him. Why is this? One reason might be that this world is a gigantic battlefield with wounded all around. All our fellow men are half dead. Their sores – physical, psychological, and spiritual – cry out to us. To look the other way is to hate our neighbour.

But that cannot be the main thing. If it were we might get along nicely in heaven while ignoring those around us. In heaven we shall have no bleeding neighbours. Yet we shall still love. Indeed, we shall love as though we had never loved before. Paul could see no end to love (1 Corinthians 13:13). Whatever else we shall do in heaven, we shall love.

Why, then, does God call it hatred when we go on our way without aiming to do our neighbour good? I have my ideas, but I am not sure they would help you. Trying to answer that question might prove interesting, but it cannot be necessary. What we must know is clear enough: if we do not love our neighbour we hate him – even if we do not dislike him at all.

And if we do not love God we hate Him. The world of unconverted men, Jesus tells us, hates Him. It hates

His Father as well. We must not be put off by the fact that the world does not yet profess to dislike God. Dislike comes with contact, with confrontation. Most men do not yet know Him well enough to dislike Him. But they will.

If we hate a *man* we are likely to come to dislike him as well, especially if we are often thrown into contact with him in his need. We will rationalize our hatred. We will excuse our neglect. It is not hard at all. We will take a simple step to do it. We will take exception to how he does business, or the hours he keeps, or the way he puts on airs, or the manners of his sons and his wife, and so on, until our thorough dislike soothes our conscience and justifies our hatred. You know this road. It is the way to hell. And most of us have been further down it than we would care to admit.

The same holds true towards God. Of course, God has no 'needs'. But He has something that will answer the purpose just as well. He has commands. His commands demand attention, just as the needs of others do. As long as men have vague ideas of God they only hate Him. That is, they ignore Him as Lord and God of their lives. They pursue their own affairs. They do their own thing. They will have a truce with God if He will let them alone. In return they may even have warm feelings towards Him. But let them once run head-on into His demands, His 'thou shalt' and His 'thou shalt not', and now all is changed. Now God is unreasonable and unfair, they say. Or, petty and peevish. Or, imperious and despotic. Yes, all of these and more.

This is the way the natural man's mind works. The antipathy to God is there all along. It is there waiting to show itself. Paul puts it this way: 'The carnal mind is enmity against God: for it is not subject to the law of God, neither indeed can be' (Romans 8:7). Man hates God as God, as King. Not as Benevolence or Love or Compassion, but as God. The natural man's mind is the enemy of God.

So now we begin to see the answer to the question with which we started this section. That question was: 'What kind of man desires to turn to God?' Or, 'What kind of man is inclined to turn to Christ?' The answer of Scripture is this. No man left to himself, no natural man, will do so. Why? Because all hate God. Yet we know that some men *do* embrace Christ. Who are these men? The only man who will turn to God is a man who has had his hatred of God removed. That kind and no other will desire to turn to God. That kind and no other will embrace Christ.

2: *Seeing and Hearing*

Let us look at our dilemma again. The Scripture commands men to turn to Christ. The same Scripture assures us that men hate God and will not come to Him. So it comes to this: a man must have his hatred of God removed or perish for ever. This is one way to look at man and it is a biblical way. In this chapter I want to look at man in another way. This way of looking at man will be biblical too, for the Scriptures show us man from many angles.

Remember that our basic question is: 'Is faith – that faith which turns to and embraces Christ – the gift of God?' One way to begin to get at the answer is to glance at this well-known text: 'So then faith cometh by hearing, and hearing by the word of God' (Romans 10:17). Paul's point here seems plain. Faith comes to us by our hearing of the gospel message, the message that comes from God and tells us of Jesus Christ. No one can put his faith in this good news unless he has heard it. Once he has heard it he may accept it or reject it, but he certainly will not accept it unless he has heard it. This is so obvious that I need not labour Paul's point.

But something else needs to be said. It is this: there is hearing and then there is hearing. Let me illustrate. Let's say that you have a friend that you would like to take along on a trip. So you try to convince your friend.

You mention the splendid scenery you hope to see. You point out your friend's need of rest and relaxation. You drop a hint that you are prepared to bear the major part of the cost. Yet your friend is unmoved. He will not go. Finally, in telling me about it you say, 'Bill was *deaf* to all my pleas.' Or as we sometimes say, 'He wouldn't *hear* of it.' Obviously the words 'deaf' and 'hear' have a different sense in this case from that which we normally attach to them. They convey the idea that Bill would not consider the trip at all. Did he hear your proposal? Yes and no. His ears caught your sounds. He heard it in that sense. But his mind rejected what his ears caught. So we say, 'He wouldn't hear of it.' In that sense, he was deaf.

We use words about sight in the same way. When you learn a new and important truth you may exclaim, 'I was *blind* to that before, but I *see* it now!' Of course you are not talking about your eyes at all in such a statement. You are describing an effect on your mind. Once you did not understand; now you do.

The Bible uses words for seeing and hearing in much the same way as we do. It is necessary for us to hear the gospel preached or see it written down in order for us to respond to it. No one, I think, doubts that. But more is needed. We must *see* it and *hear* it in other ways as well. In this chapter I want us to find out what those ways are.

Let us start with 'seeing'. Do you remember how Jesus once described the Pharisees? He said, 'They be blind leaders of the blind' (Matthew 15:14). He meant that the Pharisees were without understanding, and so were their followers. That is, they did not understand the Scriptures. To borrow Paul's phrase, 'When Moses is read, the vail is upon their heart' (2 Corinthians 3:15). These Pharisees had read the Scriptures. They carried verses from it with them. More importantly, they had memorized key portions. Yet, they were blind, Jesus said. They did not understand what they read and recited. As intelligent men they sought to grasp what they read, and no doubt they thought that they had done so. But they were blind without knowing it – the worst kind of blindness of all!

The Pharisees, of course, are no longer with us. In many ways they were creatures of their age. Their time has come and gone, and they are gone with it. In one important way, however – their blindness – they were like people of other times. We must not think that they were blind because they were Pharisees. Quite the opposite! They were Pharisees because they were blind!

The question naturally arises, Who are the blind men of history? If the Pharisees are like others in the 5th century, or the 10th, or the 20th, whom are they like? One possible answer might be: they are like the Jews of each succeeding century. After all, doesn't Paul describe the Jews in general as blind? When I quoted Paul about the vail on the heart I quoted words that were spoken of the Jewish people, not simply of the Pharisees. Is this our answer, then?

It might seem so. Certainly Paul thought of his fellow countrymen as blind. John also had these hard things to say of them:

> But though [Jesus] had done so many miracles before them, yet they believed not on him: that the saying of Esaias the prophet might be fulfilled, which he spake,

Lord, who hath believed our report? and to whom hath the arm of the Lord been revealed?

Therefore they could not believe, because that Esaias said again, He hath blinded their eyes, and hardened their heart; that they should not see with their eyes, nor understand with their heart, and be converted, and I should heal them (John 12:37-40).

Here also we see the blindness of Israel.

Yet if we focus on Israel we shall lose the larger truth that the New Testament teaches. That truth is this: *our whole race is blind*. The natural man is born blind. He lives blind. And he dies blind. The Jews had no corner on blindness. They were blind. But not because they were Jews. They were blind because they were fallen men, members of our fallen race. Through Adam's sin intense darkness covers the face of humanity. It is true that the Lord Jesus sometimes singles out His countrymen – especially the leaders – for rebuke because of their blindness. He treats them as men who are squeezing their eyelids shut lest the slightest glimmer of light should get in. And it was punished by God with yet greater blindness. Still, these Jewish leaders were but the grossest and handiest illustration of the blindness of the world at large. All men are blind, whether they inhabit Palestine or Pittsburgh, whether they belong to the 1st century or the 20th.

How do I know this? Well, it did not come naturally to me to learn it. I was taught it by God's Word. I see it, for instance, in the commission given to the Lord Jesus:

I the LORD have called thee in righteousness, and will hold thine hand, and will keep thee, and give thee for a covenant of the people, for a *light* of the Gentiles; *to open the blind eyes*, to bring out the prisoners from the prison, and *them that sit in darkness* out of the prison house (Isaiah 42:6,7).

Note the phrases I have put in italics. Here is the heart of Jesus' ministry. Men are said to be blind or in darkness (these are two ways of saying the same thing). Jesus is sent to dispel the darkness, to give sight to the blind. As 'light' He comes, not only to Jews ('the people'), but to Gentiles as well. That implies that both groups, all men, are blind or in darkness. All men are without understanding. In Paul's words, 'There is none that understandeth' (Romans 3:11). Spiritual blindness is the common condition of the human race.

But more must be said. You and I must not suppose that the simple fact that Christ came has changed this. We must not say, 'The light has come and now men see.' However desirable that may seem, it is not so. The physical presence of Christ was not enough, for 'men loved darkness (blindness) rather than light' (John 3:19). You see, I am sure, that John made this comment after Jesus had come. In fact, John tells us, this is the way men reacted to Christ's coming. They preferred darkness. They preferred blindness. Evil men, natural men, men as they come into this world, always do. The picture is humanly hopeless. Darkness in all men, and men love to have it so!

This accounts for the commission Jesus later gave to Paul. 'I have appeared unto thee,' Paul heard Jesus say, 'to make thee a minister . . . delivering thee from the people and from the Gentiles, unto whom I now send thee, to open their eyes, and to turn them from darkness to light' (Acts 26:16–18). This is the same commission Jesus received. Paul's ministry was an extension of Jesus' own ministry. The work is the same because men are the same. They need their eyes opened. All of them, without exception, are in darkness. They cannot see.

But let us leave 'seeing' and take up 'hearing'. Earlier I said that men must hear the gospel with their ears, but in other ways also. 'Hearing' like 'seeing' is used in Scripture in more than one sense. 'Hearing' may mean taking hold of truth, understanding truth, embracing and obeying truth. More than once Jesus said, 'He that hath ears to hear, let him hear' (see, for example, Matthew 11:15 and 13:43). The people He was speaking to were surely listening and hearing in the literal sense. If they had not been doing so there would have been no point in speaking to them at all. Some of them may have been listening intently, hearing every word. Even Jesus' enemies hung upon His words, sometimes praising them, but more often ridiculing them (Luke 4:22, 28, 29). They heard them all right, in the literal sense of the word. Yet, in another sense, they were deaf to the words of Christ.

In John 9 we find the story of a man, blind from birth, who was healed by the Lord Jesus. I want to quote a part of his story. Note the different uses the once blind man makes of the word 'hear'. He is being interviewed (cross-examined!) by the Pharisees.

> Then said they to him again, What did he to thee? how opened he thine eyes? He answered them, I have told you already, and ye did not *hear*: wherefore would ye *hear* it again? will ye also be his disciples? Then they reviled him, and said, Thou art his disciple; but we are Moses' disciples. (John 9:26–28)

The word 'hear' occurs twice in the man's statement, but what does it mean? Let us take a look at his second use of the word. Earlier he had told the Pharisees about his healing. Now he says, 'Wherefore would ye hear it again?' They wanted him to go through his story one more time. They wanted to hear it again in the literal sense of the word 'hear'. There is nothing unusual in this.

It is his other use of the word *hear* that attracts us and calls for comment. 'I have told you already,' he says, 'and ye did not *hear*.' What can this mean? He knows very well that they have listened carefully once before to his whole account (men who want to find something to criticize often listen carefully). Plainly the healed man has something else in mind when he says, 'Ye did not *hear*!' He means, evidently, that they would not believe him. They would not lay hold of the truth that he had indeed been born blind and had received his sight. They did not understand. Here he was, experiencing the wonder of seeing for the first time in his life, and they were utterly incapable of entering into his joy! They wouldn't hear of it!

Of course, if we had been there that day we also might have found it difficult to accept what he said. After all, one does not see a blind man healed every day. But the story of this man's healing is included in the Gospel of John to highlight the greatness of the Lord Jesus and to show the way the Jewish leaders reacted to that greatness. They were 'blind' and 'deaf' to the glory of Christ. They listened intently to the healed man just as they listened intently to Christ, but they would not embrace the truth that they had before their very eyes. 'Why do ye not understand my speech?' Jesus asked them on another occasion. Then he answered His own question: 'Even because ye *cannot* hear my word' (John 8:43). Now a man who 'cannot hear' is deaf. So Jesus was saying that they were deaf to the truth of God. Once again, they did not know they were deaf – the worst kind of deafness of all!

Earlier, in talking to you about 'seeing', I showed you that the blindness of the Jewish leaders was not unique. We found that the Jewish people as a group were also said to be blind. And what was said of them was true of all men. All men were blind to God's truth. All men need their eyes opened so that they may see. This is the plain teaching of Scripture.

We might follow the same outline in discussing 'hearing'. The Jewish leaders, as we have seen, were deaf to the truth Christ taught. Note again His emphatic statement: 'Ye *cannot* hear my word!'

But what of the Jews as a whole? And what of the world at large? Are they deaf as well as blind? I think it is clear by now that the deafness and the blindness refer to the same thing. If the Jewish leaders are blind they are deaf also. So too are the Jewish people. So is the world at large. No man is spiritually blind yet able to hear. Look with me at a passage where this can be seen, the passage where Isaiah the prophet receives his commission.

> And [God] said, Go, and tell this people, Hear ye indeed, but understand not; and see ye indeed, but perceive not. Make the heart of this people fat, and make their ears heavy, and shut their eyes; *lest they see with their eyes, and hear with their ears, and understand with their heart*, and convert, and be healed (Isaiah 6:9, 10).

Does this passage sound familiar? John quotes it in his Gospel, chapter 12. We looked at his use of it when we were discussing 'seeing'. For some reason it did not serve John's purpose there to quote the words about hearing, so he omitted them. Probably he left them out because he was talking about Jesus' miracles at that point. The miracles, of course, struck the eyes of men much more than their ears.

These verses from Isaiah 6 show us that 'seeing' and 'hearing' and 'understanding with the heart' all mean the same thing. If men do not see, they do not hear. If they do not hear, they do not understand with the heart. 'There is none that understandeth' applies to hearing as well as to seeing. If all men are blind – and they are – then all men are deaf also. *All men are deaf* – Jews and Gentiles, rich and poor, slave and free.

Now let us try to relate these facts about seeing and hearing to what we learned about man in the first chapter of this book. There I wrote:

So now we begin to see the answer to the question with which we started this section. That question was: 'What kind of man desires to turn to God?' Or, 'What kind of man is inclined to turn to Christ?' The answer of Scripture is this: no man left to himself, no natural man will do so. Why? Because all hate God. Yet we know that some men *do* embrace Christ. Who are these men? The only man who will turn to God is a man who has had his hatred of God removed. That kind and no other will desire to turn to God. That kind and no other will embrace Christ.

Do you see that by replacing the idea of 'hatred of God' with the idea of 'lack of understanding' that same paragraph would sum up what I have said in this chapter? Let me try it.

'What kind of man is inclined to turn to Christ? The

answer of Scripture is: no man left to himself, no natural man, will do so. Why? Because all are deaf and blind. Because all are without understanding. Yet we know that some men *do* embrace Christ. Who are these men? The only man who will turn to God is a man who has had his blindness, his deafness, his lack of understanding removed. That kind and no other will desire to turn to God. That kind and no other will embrace Christ.'

The Scripture teaches, then, that at least two things keep all natural men from Christ. First, there is their hatred of God. Second, there is their lack of understanding. Either would prove fatal. So, something must be done to remove these obstacles to faith. A bit later we will talk about what that 'something' is. For now it is enough to understand the dilemma.

A thought just occurs to me. I imagine you, the reader, saying to me something like this: 'Isn't it quite unfair that a man's lack of understanding should keep him from Christ? Hatred of God is one thing. I can see how that would shut him away from the Saviour. But lack of understanding? Somehow that doesn't seem right.'

And I imagine you raising another objection, too, something like this: 'And besides, compared to hatred of God, lack of understanding can't be so serious. Isn't bringing in blindness and deafness at this point a bit of an anticlimax?' And good questions they are!

The answer to these questions lies in a fact that you have seen in the Bible, but perhaps have not paid particular attention to it. That fact is this: the Bible frequently blames men for their lack of understanding. It treats men as blameworthy when they are blind and deaf to truth. The writers of Scripture look at men as creatures who 'ought to know'. In other words, ignorance is a moral issue with them. It is a matter of right and wrong. When Jesus called the Pharisees 'blind leaders of the blind' that was not a mere observation. It was much more than that! It was a judgment of the severest kind.

How do we account for this? Well, we must not kick at it. We must not try to ignore it. It is precisely here where the shoe pinches, as we say, that we can take a large step forward in our own understanding of Scripture. For the Lord Jesus' judgments are always right and just and true.

What is there that is blameworthy in lack of understanding? *That will depend on why it exists*. The lack that the Scripture rebukes comes from a lack of sympathy with the Author of Scripture and His interests. It is what we call *bias*. It is not that innocent, expectant lack of understanding that lights up the face of a little child eager to learn. It is, rather, settled antagonism. That is what it is. But we may not see it for what it is because we expect opposition to God to show itself in a different way. We expect to see it in a man's passions. If a man stands in a bar room and entertains his friends by angrily cursing God we suppose that he is hostile to God. And so he is. But most of us have never shown our hostility to God in that way. Nor will we.

Some men's hostility to God works itself out through their emotions. True enough! But every man's antagonism to God works itself out through his mind. 'The carnal mind is enmity against God' (Romans 8:7). The only mind that the natural man has is a mind set against the truth of God. His lack of understanding is not an innocent thing. In fact, his lack of understanding

35

is not something new to us. It is just another side of the subject of our last chapter, another side of his hatred of God.

And so it comes to this: some power must intervene to rescue man from himself. See how Paul views man's plight. 'The natural man,' he says, 'receiveth not the things of the Spirit of God: for they are foolishness unto him' (1 Corinthians 2:14). Paul does *not* say, 'the deep things of God' (I feel sure that I read it that way, though, for years). No, Paul is emphatic. The natural man receives *nothing* of God's truth, because it is folly to him. No man stakes his life, his destiny, on foolishness. Some power must make him see God's Word for what it is, the truth of God, or he must perish eternally.

The question is: Where will man find this power?

3: *Power*

What we want is power. It seems almost ridiculous to write a sentence saying *that*, when we live in an age of power undreamed of by men of the past. Haven't we harnessed the power of the atom? Yet it is still true that we lack power. What we have is an abundance of physical power. What we need is power of quite another kind.

Let us look at our dilemma again. The Scripture commands men to turn to Christ. The same Scripture assures us that men hate God. It says, too, that they do not understand God's truth. These things keep them from God. So it comes to this: a man must have his hatred of God removed and his eyes and ears opened, or he must perish for ever. Power to do this is needed. The question comes back: where will man find this power?

In this chapter I want to take up one common answer to this question. That answer is: *man has the power within himself*. And I want you to take that answer seriously. Why? For this reason: Christians, I believe, have been trained not to take this answer seriously *when it is stated in this way* (in the next chapter we will put it another way). When it is stated in this way it seems to contradict too much of what they have learned. And so, many reject this solution right off, when it is put this way.

Do not misunderstand me. In the end I shall reject this answer also. I am sure we must if we want to be true to God's Word. But we must not reject this answer when it is put this way, only to accept it when it meets us in another form. For I feel sure that that is what many of us have been taught to do, as I hope to show later. Right now, however, we will concentrate on it in this form. Does man have the power within himself to remove his hatred of God? Can he take away his own blindness and deafness?

To ask these questions is almost to answer them. Yet God's Word must again be allowed to speak for itself. We shall find that the Scripture speaks to this question in two ways. First, it paints man as a weakling. Second, it shows us man as a slave, under the domination of sin and Satan.

The net effect of these two views of man is the same. You may think of man as without power, or you may think of him as having power that is made ineffectual because something or someone much more powerful is holding him in bondage. *In either case he is helpless.*

Let us look at man's helplessness. We will take Romans 5:6–8 as our starting point.

> For when we were yet without strength, in due time Christ died for the ungodly. For scarcely for a righteous man will one die: yet peradventure for a good man some would even dare to die. But God commendeth his love toward us, in that, while we were yet sinners, Christ died for us.

In these three verses are five descriptions of us men. Two are implied and three are spelled out for us. It is plainly implied that we men are not righteous men and we are not good men. If we had been, Paul tells us, Christ's death could be easily explained. From time to time some man lays down his life to save the life of another whom he takes to be a good man. We understand that. But, Paul says, that is not what happened in our case. Christ died for men who were 'without strength', 'ungodly', and 'sinners'.

Now here is an odd thing. It seems clear, doesn't it, that in order for a man to be ungodly and sinful he has to have some strength. To curse God uses energy. To murder and to gossip, to steal and to seduce, all require power. But this seeming contradiction is the key to Paul's meaning. It is not every kind of strength that Paul has in mind. He is looking at spiritual strength, the power to break off from ungodly, sinful ways. In this respect men were 'without strength' when Jesus died. They had no power *within* that would snap the bonds of sin and Satan.

Paul and the writer of Hebrews make this same point in another striking way. They talk about the weakness of the law. What does this have to do with our own weakness? Let us look at what they say, and then we will come back to this question.

> Is the law then against the promises of God? God forbid: for if there had been a law given which could have given life, verily righteousness should have been by the law. (Galatians 3:21)
>
> For there is verily a disannulling of the commandment going before for the weakness and unprofitableness thereof. (Hebrews 7:18)
>
> The law . . . was weak through the flesh. (Romans 8:3)

The general idea in each of these passages is the same. The law could not do something we might have expected it to do. It could not make men right with God. Nor could it move men to act in a godly way. The law was weak and unprofitable for these ends.

Now why was the law weak? Was the law bad? Not at all! The law was 'holy, and just, and good' (Romans 7:12). The law's problem was not in itself. Its problem lay in the material it had to work on. Paul calls that material 'the flesh', that is, fallen human nature. 'The law was weak through the flesh.' The law was fine. The material was hopeless, so far as the law was concerned. Human nature was too much for the law. If anything was to be done, something more than the law would have to do it.

The law was strong to command. But then it was baffled by the weakness of the flesh it commanded. 'Do this!' it said. 'Do that!' The law barked orders to its troops, but the troops were listless. The law had no power to give them, and they had none of their own. The orders were grand, but the troops were dead on their feet. So the weakness and helplessness of the law turns out to be the weakness and helplessness of human nature. In simplest terms, natural men cannot obey God.

But there is more to be said. Paul continues to speak. In other places he puts the whole question of our strength in the most startling way, so that we cannot mistake his meaning. 'You were dead,' Paul tells the Ephesians, in a passage that is quite as suited to you, and to me, and to every man who has ever lived, as it was to those first-century readers. Dead! That is the end of the line. When weakness reaches death life's journey is over. It has run its course. Nothing is more helpless than a corpse.

We must look at this death more closely. Here are Paul's words in context:

> And you hath he quickened [i.e., made alive], who were dead in trespasses and sins; wherein in time past ye walked according to the course of this world, according to the prince of the power of the air, the spirit that now worketh in the children of disobedience; among whom also we all had our conversation in times past in the lusts of our flesh, fulfilling the desires of the flesh and of the mind; and were by nature the children of wrath, even as others. (Ephesians 2:1-3)

I think you will agree with me that this is a strange description of death. These dead men walk and talk. They look anything but helpless. This demands examination. What did Paul mean?

Perhaps an analogy will help us. In a crowded room, buzzing with conversation, a young lady sits to one side, a distant look in her eyes. She has just received news. Her fiancé, thought to have been lost in battle, is alive and returning to her. What a reunion that will be! She can think of nothing else. She hears none of the small talk around her. A friend, waving from across the room, will not get her attention. She is insensible to her surroundings. They have no charms for her. To them she is dead.

You see that the young lady points up a law of our being. In order to be alive to some things we must be dead to others. You see, too, that in order for her to be dead to those around her she had to be intensely, one might say 'electrically', alive to something else; in this case to the news that engaged her mind. I called the conversation in the room 'small talk'. But it need not have been small talk at all. It might have been on stirring themes or the most urgent affairs of state. No matter! She was dead to it all, so that she might be fully alive to the thought of her lover's return. Our English idiom recognizes this kind of insensibility as a 'death' by writing over it, 'Buried in Thought!'

Now, I think, we are better able to follow Paul. When he writes about death here he is writing about insensibility towards God. In this sense, the natural man is dead to God. But he does not manage this 'death' by lying down and folding his hands. Just the opposite! He maintains this death by being intensely alive to the things Paul lists here. He 'lives' for this world and Satan ('the prince of the power of the air') and his own desires. His hands and heart and mind are full. He concentrates on these things as the young lady concentrated on her lover.

One wonders if the word 'pre-occupied' was coined just to describe the natural man. Something 'occupied' him before God, so to speak. So much already occupies every nook and cranny of his being that there is no room for God. He is a study in insensibility on one hand and in concentration on the other.

And that brings us round again to helplessness. For, make no mistake about it, concentration in one direction makes us helpless in another. Just suppose for the moment that you were the one in the room with the young lady waving to get her attention.

'Didn't you see me?' you ask.

'No,' she says.

'But I was right in front of you, right in your line of sight. How could you miss me?'

'I don't know.'

'Are you sure you didn't see me?' This time your voice betrays irritation. But there is no reason to be offended. She did not see you. It was nothing personal. She could not see you. She was as unable to see you at that moment as she would have been if she had covered her eyes. No, more! She was as helpless as she would have been if she had been stone blind. 'Dead' is not too strong a word.

As far as it goes the figure of the corpse, as used by the Apostle, tells the story as it ought to be told. As we have seen, however, it shows helplessness in a way that may seem divorced from reality. Lost men, of course, are living, breathing creatures. With this in mind the Lord Jesus used another likeness to bring home the truth of man's helplessness. He used the likeness of the slave. We must look at that next.

> Then said Jesus to those Jews which believed on him, If ye continue in my word, then are ye my disciples indeed; and ye shall know the truth, and the truth shall make you free.
>
> They answered him, We be Abraham's seed, and were never in bondage to any man; how sayest thou, Ye shall be made free?
>
> Jesus answered them, Verily, verily, I say unto you, Whosoever committeth sin is the servant of sin. And the servant abideth not in the house for ever: but the Son abideth ever. If the Son therefore shall make you free, ye shall be free indeed. (John 8:31-6)

It strikes us, first of all, that this passage is not directly concerned with Jesus' worst critics. In fact, in it He speaks to men who, in some sense, 'believed on him' (v.31). We need to know this so that we do not set aside what Jesus says, as though He did not mean to apply it to all natural men. At this point he is not addressing extreme cases. If those who 'believed on him' were slaves, so must all men be. With this in mind we can look at the scene more closely.

The subject is: slavery and freedom. Jesus opens by offering freedom to slaves. Then conflict begins. His listeners tell Jesus that they cannot see how this offer fits their position. If Jesus means this gift for them He has obviously misjudged their situation. They are free men! That is the only way they can see it.

Yet the Lord Jesus is not put off by this. He presses upon them their bondage. Whoever practises sin, He says, is a slave. A man who practises sin may think his sin serves himself, but he is mistaken. The master is sin; the slave is the sinner. The fact that a man does not feel his bondage does not change things one whit. Sinners – and that includes all natural men – are slaves to sin, however loudly they trumpet their fancied freedom. Their freedom is bondage; their liberty is illusion. It may seem hard to think that a man may be a slave and still suppose that he is free. But the case is much like blindness and deafness. Can a man be blind and still think that he can see? Can he be deaf and still think that he can hear? We have seen the answers to these questions already. The worst kind of blindness and deafness and slavery is the kind that one does not feel. Men sit chained in the prison of sin, yet imagine themselves free. What worse bondage could there be?

But is 'prison' the right word? Let us look at Jesus' commission once more.

> I the LORD have called thee in righteousness, and will hold thine hand, and will keep thee, and give thee for a covenant of the people, for a light of the Gentiles; to open the blind eyes, *to bring out the prisoners from the prison*, and them that sit in darkness *out of the prison house*. (Isaiah 42:6, 7)

(I quoted this earlier, but this time I have italicized different words).

The picture here is the picture of the natural man in a dungeon, a place where light does not penetrate. We do not learn whether he is happy or unhappy. We are not told if he is aware of his state. The point lies elsewhere. It is this. He will stay in prison until he is taken out. There are no escapes. No prisoner is clever enough to find his way out. The Lord Jesus will 'bring out the prisoners', or they will not come out at all. Yes, 'prison' is the right word indeed.

And there is more. We learn a new fact when Paul receives the same commission. We learn that this prison has a jailer. Here are Jesus' words to Paul:

> I have appeared unto thee for this purpose, to make thee a minister . . . delivering thee from the people, and from the Gentiles, unto whom now I send thee, to open their eyes, and to turn them from darkness to light, and from the power of Satan unto God. (Acts 26:16–18)

You will see my point by comparing this with Isaiah 42:7 above. Note the phrase 'from the power of Satan' here. Compare it with 'out of the prison house' there. They are parallel. Each is a commentary on the other. If we ask, 'Who is the prison keeper?' the answer is, 'Satan.' If we ask, 'What is this prison?' the answer is, 'The power to keep men in darkness.' To get out of the prison is to get out from under the authority of Satan. To be under his power is to be a slave. So man is a slave to sin and to Satan. Not just to one, but to both.

In his ministry Paul does not forget this. Such facts as these form the starting-point of Paul's preaching of salvation. His message is addressed to slaves (in this he follows his Master). At one point he speaks of men as 'dead in sins' (Ephesians 2:1). In the next breath, however, he speaks of them as very much alive, but under the thumb of 'the prince of the power of the air', Satan (2:2). Paul feels no difficulty in saying both these things. His point is the same in each case. You may think of man, he is telling us, in one of two ways. You may think of him as helpless, without power. Or, if you prefer, you may think of him as having a good deal of power. But, Paul warns us, if you say that man has power you must always say something else too. You must add that, whatever power man has, be it little or much, is under the control of Satan. All of it! In other words, you must never forget to say that *man is a slave*.

And so we have come round to the place we foresaw at the beginning of this chapter. We have rejected the notion that man has power *within* himself to change his life. But we have done it, I think, for the right reason. It has not been done because we have been programmed to do it by our religious background. Rather, the Scripture leaves us little choice.

To be fair with Scripture we must see man as God sees him. We may say that man is helpless, even dead, or we may say that he is a slave to forces more powerful than himself. In either view he has no power to do what must be done. He has no power to remove his hatred of God. He has no strength to take away his own blindness and deafness.

So the question of man's *power* would seem to be settled. Powerlessness, not power, pertains to man. But what if those who are not convinced of this, claim that man possesses the power of 'free will'. Will that change anything?

4: *'Free Will'*

If man has no power, what about this thing called 'free will?' That seems to be the question that must come to everyone's mind in this connection, sooner or later. So, it is time to take it up.

I want to start by repeating something I said in the last chapter. I told you there that I would reject the idea that man has power within himself to change himself. I went on to say that I am sure that we must reject this idea

'. . . if we want to be true to God's Word. But we must not reject this answer when it is put this way, only to accept it when it meets us in another form. For I feel sure that that is what many of us have been taught to do . . .'

Well, the new form is 'free will'. And now is the time to see whether that is true. But first we shall need a definition.

What, then, is meant by free will? I will not, you understand, attempt anything like a scientific definition. What we are after is what the ordinary man means when he talks about free will. The word 'will', I think, should be reasonably clear for our purposes. I am taking it to mean 'the power of choice'. When one fellow takes vanilla ice cream and another chooses apple-pie, each has exercised his will. Each has made his choice. I do not think that we can go far wrong here. Part of being what God made us – real men and not puppets on a string – is having the power to choose. We need not deny that. But what about this word 'free'? What is *free* will?

The only way to answer this question seems to be to ask another: 'Free from what?' And here the possibilities overwhelm us. Free from God? Free from Satan? Free from heredity? Free from culture, or environment? Free from training? And we could go on and on. There seems to be no end to what one might mean in asking this question. A whole library of books would be required to answer it.

Our way out is to narrow the question. Let me just ask this: 'Is the will of man free from what the man himself is?' There is the question for us.

Now we sometimes meet people who say, 'Of course men have free will. Just look at Adam and Eve.' They mean that man's will – his power of choice – is the same as it was before Adam and Eve sinned. Every man, they say, can choose as Adam and Eve did. But is this true? Did the entrance of sin and man's fall bring no change to man's will? Can he now choose in either a godly or an ungodly direction? Doesn't all of our experience go to show that men's wills are tied to what they themselves are? They choose to act in a way that matches what their hearts are like. And that holds true even when they choose to act in a way that baffles us, as they often do. We still feel sure that there is some part of their make-up that would explain their choices if we could only get at it. If Mary Brown steals from me, I think of something more than her act. I think I have discovered some flaw in her character as well. I am sure that what she chooses to do reveals a bit of what she is. In fact, we call a man 'insane' whose known character does not explain his choices. And we do it in order to connect what he is with what he does. We simply cannot get along without making this connection!

But let us move on, as we look further at this point, to ask, What does the Scripture say? And first, what has the Lord Jesus said? Let us look at His words in Matthew 12:33-35.

> Either make the tree good, and his fruit good; or else make the tree corrupt, and his fruit corrupt; for the tree is known by his fruit. O generation of vipers, how can ye, being evil, speak good things? For out of the abundance of the heart the mouth speaketh. A good man out of the good treasure of the heart bringeth forth good things: and an evil man out of the evil treasure bringeth forth evil things.

More than once our Lord Jesus compared men to trees (see also Matthew 7:15-20 and Luke 6:43-45). Men are like trees in this way: their acts show what they are like inside, just as fruit reveals the quality of the tree. If you find good fruit you know you have found a good tree. If you find godly deeds you know you have found a godly man. And the opposite is true too. Worthless fruit comes from worthless trees. Ungodly acts come from ungodly men. The point is clear. Men's deeds (and words) reflect what men are. A man's deeds are of the same quality as the man himself.

But the terse way Jesus puts this raises two difficulties. The first is this. Jesus' comparison seems to leave no room for hypocrites, people who hide what they really are. Now, of course, Jesus was aware of such people. The fact that they exist will help us to grasp

Jesus' meaning. He does not mean that we can uncover a man's make-up by a glance at a single act. God does that. We cannot. We are wrong, terribly wrong, to try. Sooner or later, however, a hypocrite's acts generally will give him away. Jesus gives clues to hypocrisy all through the Gospels. We do well to find them and to apply them, especially to ourselves!

A second thing needs clearing up. It is this. The men we see around us do not seem to fit neatly into either mould. Most of them we would think of as neither godly nor ungodly. We wonder why the Lord Jesus speaks in extremes, of good trees and corrupt trees, when all the men we know seem to be a mixture of good and evil. We are sure He has His reasons, but what are they?

In the passage I have quoted (Matthew 12:33–35) one reason is brought to light. Jesus has Himself in view. In the context the Pharisees hear of Jesus' good works and, of course, have to explain them. So they say that Jesus' works, which they admit are good, are done by Satan's power. No, says Jesus, that option is not open to you. You must either consider Me good and My works good, or consider Me evil and My works evil. You cannot separate these things.

Now this was a natural way for Jesus to speak of Himself, since He knew Himself to be absolutely good. In the Lord Jesus there was no mixture of evil at all.

There are still other reasons why the Lord Jesus spoke in extremes. Since we are thinking about free will we will concentrate on one of them that touches our subject. It is this. Everything that a natural man does is sinful. The natural man is an evil man. His deeds match his heart. What he does goes along with what he is. *His case is an extreme case*, though it may not seem such to us. And that means that this was the true way for the Lord to speak of lost men as well.

I must not pass over this too quickly. If you feel uncomfortable with the idea that everything the natural man does is sinful I am not surprised. Still, it is true. It is true for this reason: an act is not an isolated thing. It does not stand alone. The deed and the reason for the deed, its motive(s), are a unit. They both come from the man. They are bound up together like the light and heat from a candle. You dare not separate them. But if you search into them together, as God does, you will find the same chunk of ugliness that God finds. However pure the act may seem, you will find it poisoned by hatred of God. God's first command to us is to love Him with all that we are. All else is to flow from that. And that is exactly what the natural man will not do. That is his fatal flaw. The stream of his life is polluted all the way down, because it is polluted at its source. All that he does, however magnificent, bears the impress of his rebellion. We must pay attention to this; God does.

We are ready now to return to the Lord Jesus with His trees and fruit. From what we have said above we know that we want to look particularly at the corrupt tree and the corrupt fruit. Why? Because that tree pictures the natural man. It is in the natural man that some men hope to find a will free from what the man himself is. Let us see whether the Lord Jesus has left any room for free will in that sense.

Where does the will come into the picture Jesus has drawn? There are, it seems, three possibilities. (1) We may think of the will as being a part of what the man is, a part of the tree, if you please. (2) We may think of the will as being a part of what the man does, a part of the fruit. (3) We may think of the will as standing between what a man is and what he does. In fact, I think this is the way, rightly or wrongly, we most often regard our wills. These three ways would seem to be the only roads open to our consideration.

Now we see at once, do we not, that neither (1) nor (2) leaves any room for a will that is free in the way we are talking about. If the will is part of the tree, part of what the natural man is, it is corrupt just as he is. And things are no better if we make it part of the fruit, part of what he does. For, Jesus tells us, the fruit is corrupt also. Either way the natural man's will is bound to what he is. It is corrupt. There is no place for free will (in the special sense we are seeking it) here. If we are to find the kind of free will we are looking for, it would seem that we are shut up to (3).

In (3) above I suggested that we often think of our wills as standing between what we are and what we do. Something like this:

    a. I am a man
    b. I will an act
    c. I act

That is the sequence we have in mind. (It is not necessary that I defend this position. We are looking at it as a possibility.) Suppose it is so. Then what? Will it leave the will free from what the man is? Let us see.

Again we must hear the Lord Jesus. 'Make the tree corrupt, and his fruit corrupt,' He says, 'for the tree is known by his fruit.' Jesus is telling us that it makes no difference where you place the will in relation to the man and his deeds. Things will come out the same. *A man's deeds will always be of the same moral quality as the man*. Put his will wherever you please. If you place the will between the man and his deeds nothing will change. The will does not alter the moral quality of the deeds. When the man is evil his acts are evil too.

Let me close this chapter by making some comparisons. How does the state of man's will relate to his hatred of God? How does it fit in with his blindness and deafness? How is it related to his helplessness? These are the things we looked at in the first three chapters.

We may say at once that the bondage of the natural man's will is a form of his helplessness. Man has no power for godliness. Call him 'free' if you care to. Call his will 'free'. But when all has been said and done he is as helpless for godliness as before. He is helpless to do a godly act. He is helpless to make a change within. He is what he is, a hater of God, a man blind to God's truth. Is he free and powerful as Adam was? Let Jeremiah answer: 'Can the Ethiopian change his skin, or the leopard his spots? Then may ye also do good, that are accustomed to do evil' (Jeremiah 13:23).

The final point to grasp is this. Man's helplessness (including the bondage of his will) is not something distinct from his hatred of God and his lack of understanding. It is another side of these things. In an earlier chapter I called it 'bias'. The natural man is biased against God. Let us hear Romans 8:7 once more: 'The carnal mind is enmity against God.' This bias, or enmity, or hatred, sets his course away from God. He goes his own way and is insensible to the other path.

In one sense there is nothing wrong with man's will. His mechanism for making choices is intact. His faculties work. He makes real choices all the time and for those choices he is responsible to God. Man's problem is of a different kind. It is not in his mechanism. It is in his disposition. He loves himself and hates his God. He asserts that love and that hatred in his choices. His every choice – if we could see as God sees – would show us his moral character. He chooses to please his ungodly self. He is bound to do so. He can do nothing else. To change he would have to be made into a new man. Can he do that to himself? To ask the question is to answer it.

5: *New Birth*

I have not forgotten our basic question: 'Is faith, that faith which turns to and embraces Christ, the gift of God?' If I seemed to lay it aside I did so to bring us to this point, the point where only one answer seems possible. For only one answer *is* possible. We are now ready for an emphatic 'Yes!' Faith is God's gift. In no degree could a natural man produce faith. It is utterly beyond him. Let us adore the God who gives it.

I want to review for a minute the steps that brought us here. First, we saw that while faith in God is necessary the natural man hates the God he must turn to. And so, he will not turn to God in faith. Second, we saw the natural man's blindness and deafness. That is, we saw that he does not understand the things of God. That does not mean that he cannot discuss them intelligently. Often he can. It means, rather, that he cannot understand how these things bear on him personally. With respect to their bearing on himself the natural man sees and hears only foolishness, not wisdom from God. Therefore he will not embrace the truth for himself.

Finally, we saw his helplessness. He is dead (insensible) towards God. God's invitations fall on his ears in vain. He is a slave to sin and to Satan. Every ounce of his strength is spent in serving them. He has no power within to turn himself. His will, with all else that he is, is a captive that needs to be set free. In other words, if the natural man is to have faith it must be bestowed on him as a gift. There is no other way. Yes, faith is a gift of God.

Now I think I see two ways, and only two, in which this gift might be given. So, in this section, I will ask you to follow me as we look at these two ways. We shall have to discard one of them, but it will still be worth looking at. It will help us to understand the other, the Biblical way by which God gives faith.

Perhaps a picture will get us started. As I am writing this, Christmas is just over. One feature of Christmas that most of us know well is the Christmas tree. I suppose I have seen dozens of them in the last few weeks. In some areas it seems that almost everyone decorates a tree for Christmas. If you think of both the tree and its ornaments you will have the picture I want to look at. I hope that you are familiar with very beautiful ornaments so that they will glisten in your mental image.

Now let me ask you a question. What is the connection between those beautiful ornaments and the tree? Do they grow on the tree? They do not. Is there any living bond between them? No, there is not. They are hung on the tree by little hooks. Or, they are tied on with bright ribbons. There is, however, no living connection between them. We might say that the ornaments are aliens. They do not belong to the tree at all.

It is possible to think of faith in much the same way. Here is the natural man. He is like the Christmas tree. He has no fruit or ornaments of his own. Then God comes along and hangs the bright jewel of faith on him.

Now he sparkles and gleams, but we must keep in mind that his faith is an alien. There is no real connection between what he is and this gift of faith from God. He is an old dry tree, but he has one ornament from the hand of Another, and that ornament dazzles us with its light.

In some ways this picture appeals to us. It certainly brings out the helplessness of man. It dramatizes the action of God too. In this picture there could be no question of man taking credit for what God does. The old dry tree has the ornament of faith solely by the hand of God. And that is the Biblical view exactly. We must guard this truth with all our might. We must not let it slip. It is a precious truth, a foundational truth. Nevertheless, it is not the whole truth. This picture is not really sound. It leaves out too much. We must reject it so that we may the better understand all that the Word of God teaches.

The Bible itself has the picture we need. In fact it has several such illustrations, as we shall see. But just now I want to concentrate on one. The picture I have in mind is birth. The Scripture calls the beginnings of our Christian life a being 'born again'. This likeness of a new birth is God's way of telling us what He does in bringing men to faith in Christ.

The trouble with the Christmas tree analogy is this. It leaves out the connection between what a man is and what he does. Faith is there, to be sure, but it is hung on the man. There is no living link between the man and his faith. In fact, there is no reason to call it *his* faith at all. It no more belongs to him than the ornament belongs to the tree. After Christmas the tree is taken away and burned. Next year the ornament will 'belong to' another tree, and the following year to still another. That is because it does not really belong to any particular tree at all.

The picture of birth leads us in another direction while holding on to the truth of man's helplessness. For, when you think of it, no event in our lives gives us less room for boasting than our birth. If we tried to take some credit for our birth others would see through our bluff in a moment. Yet the picture of birth opens the way, as we shall see, for faith from God to be really ours, while remaining His gift to us.

But first a word of caution. I am afraid we have come to think of faith and the new birth in just the opposite way that we ought to think. Let me explain what I mean. Doesn't the common idea amount to this: a man must repent of his sin and exercise faith in order to be born again? But, of course, if that were so, he would have had some part, however small, in bringing about his own birth. And that would give him something, however small, to boast about. And that, in turn, would destroy the picture of birth. If a man must repent and have faith in order to be born again – if he must make some such decision about it – then he is the cause, in part at least, of his own birth. I think it is safe to say that the world has never seen a birth like that!

No, the Biblical view is quite the opposite. Put simply, it is this. A man must be born again in order to exercise faith.[1] Perhaps we can see how this is so if we use some phrases borrowed from the Old Testament. In Ezekiel 36:26, 27 God says:

A new heart also will I give you, and a new spirit will I put within you: and I will take away the stony heart out

[1] Although this is the order of God's work in conversion it is not the order of which the convert himself is consciously aware for reasons with which I will deal later (pp. 121–122).

of your flesh, and I will give you an heart of flesh. And I will put my spirit within you, and cause you to walk in my statutes, and ye shall keep my judgments, and do them.

Now I want to lift out two phrases from these words of God through Ezekiel. God speaks of a 'stony heart' and of 'an heart of flesh'. He tells the people of Israel that in the day when He causes them to serve Him (whenever that may be) He will do it by making an exchange. Out will go the stony heart! In its place God will put an heart of flesh. Here we have God's method of getting men going in the direction He chooses – an heart transplant!

This pictures what the New Testament calls being 'born again'. Perhaps Jesus had this passage in view when He spoke to Nicodemus about the new birth. (John 3:1–9). The picture is not, of course, about our physical hearts, the organs that pump our blood. If we had stony hearts of that kind in our chests we would be corpses. The word *heart* here, as so often in Scripture, refers to what we really are, stripped of all mere appearances. Apart from the grace of God we, like Israel of old, are men of stone within. We are insensible to truth. We are dead towards God.

God's cure for this is to take away the heart of stone. He replaces it with a softer heart, a heart tender towards Himself. The change God makes is so great that it is like being born all over again. Just as the old heart went out against God in rebellion and unbelief, just so the new heart moves towards God in repentance and faith. Repentance and faith, then, are signs that the new heart is there. They are signs that the new life has come. They are the birth cries of the new creature.

They cannot precede the new birth. They must follow it. Repentance and faith do not cause the new birth. Far from it! The new birth causes repentance and faith.

And so we see how God gives faith. He gives it by giving the new heart. He does not hang it on the old natural man as you hang an ornament on the Christmas tree. God makes a new man who delights in exercising faith towards God. The new man's faith is really his own. It flows out of his new life. It is he, not God, who believes. Yet the faith is from God, a gift pure and simple. In giving the new heart God gives the faith. To God be the glory! There is nothing for man to do but to fall at His feet in wonder and adoration.

Now that we know how God gives faith we see something else we missed before. We should have seen it all along. This way of making new men is just what the New Testament might have led us to expect.

I have in mind those places that tell us why men do not come to Christ. How do the Scriptures account for this? Repeatedly they point to the heart. There's the problem, they say. More is involved than a simple choice. It is true that men do not choose Christ. But why not? Their evil hearts stand in their way. This is the root; unbelief is the fruit.

A moral change is needed for faith. Listen to these words from the Gospel of John:

This is the condemnation, that light is come into the world, and men loved darkness rather than light, because their deeds were evil. For every one that doeth evil hateth the light, neither cometh to the light, lest his deeds should be reproved. But he that doeth truth cometh to the light, that his deeds may be made manifest, that they are wrought in God. (John 3:19–21)

What have we here? A good deal more than I can comment on, of course. But two things stand out. First, there is the theme of the Lord Jesus as the light that has come into the world. This theme is continued from chapter one of John's Gospel. Second, there is the reaction of men. 'Every one that doeth evil hateth the light, neither cometh to the light.' The natural man's moral state keeps him from Christ. As an evildoer he will not come. Yet that is what he is by nature. He must be a changed man to come to the Light. It is true that John sees some men coming to the Light. But note how he accounts for this. Those who come are those who do (practise) the truth. That is, they are men, as John goes on to say, whose deeds are 'wrought in God'. They are godly people. Their lives have already been changed. It need not surprise us that there were godly men and women among the Jews before Jesus appeared. When the Lord Jesus came they were attracted to Him. I think, for instance, of Simeon and Anna (Luke 2:25–38). New men and women come to Him; others do not.

Again, notice in John 5:43, 44 how a moral change, a change at the core of the man, is needed so that men may believe. Jesus is speaking:

I am come in my Father's name, and ye receive me not; if another shall come in his own name, him ye will receive. How can ye believe, which receive honour one of another, and seek not the honour that cometh from God only?

First, Jesus makes an observation. These men did not receive Him. That was clear enough. An outsider might have seen that. They might receive others, but they would not receive Him. Second, Jesus explains why this was so. He goes beyond what an outsider, a mere bystander, might see. He looks into their hearts. There He sees an obstacle to their believing. These men sought (and got) praise from one another. That is, they were acting like natural men act. *As long as they did that they could not believe*. Some power would have to change them or they would go on in their unbelief. A moral change, Jesus tells them, is needed for faith. That, of course, goes much deeper than a simple choice, a single act of will.

We see the same thing in John 6:43–45:

> Jesus therefore answered and said unto them, Murmur not among yourselves. No man can come to me, except the Father which hath sent me draw him: and I will raise him up at the last day. It is written in the prophets, And they shall be all taught of God. Every man therefore that hath heard, and hath learned of the Father, cometh unto me.

The claims Jesus made for Himself often drew forth hostile comments. On this occasion He had said, 'I am the bread which came down from heaven' (6:41). Jesus' critics did not like the sound of that. He seemed to be making far too much of Himself. They murmured about it, and their murmurs reached His ears.

The Lord Jesus did not let their grumblings go unnoticed. On the other hand, surprisingly, He did not defend Himself by arguing. He chose rather to explain why they complained. 'No man can come to me,' He said, 'except the Father which hath sent me draw him.' That was Jesus' own explanation of their hostile words. The Father had not drawn them. But what does that mean?

Happily, we are not left to wonder. In verse forty-five Jesus gives us His meaning. His Father draws men by teaching them. Those who are taught come to Christ, every one of them. That leaves Jesus' critics on the outside. They are untaught. That is why they murmur. If the Father had taught them that Jesus was the Bread of Life they would have fed their souls on Him. Instead, they grumble.

To be sure that we catch the force of Jesus' words we must remember what we have already learned about ignorance. In our second chapter we saw that

'. . . the Bible frequently blames men for their lack of understanding. It treats men as blameworthy when they are blind and deaf to truth. The writers of Scripture look at men as creatures who "ought to know". In other words, ignorance is a moral issue with them. It is a matter of right and wrong. When Jesus called the Pharisees "blind leaders of the blind" that was not a mere observation. It was much more than that! It was a judgment of the severest kind.'

And so here also we have a word of judgment from Jesus. The Father does not draw you, Jesus tells these men (John 6:44). To them His words may have meant little or nothing. But the truth behind these words is staggering. These men loved their ignorance, and the Father was letting them have what they loved. He had not made them into new men; therefore, they would not come to Christ. Once again: a moral change is needed to believe in the Lord Jesus. It will not do to talk about a simple decision. What is needed is new life. A man must be born again in order to believe.

This truth is so important that I think we ought to see it illustrated yet once more. This time I want to turn to John chapter eight. Jesus' Jewish listeners are speaking:

> . . . We have one Father, even God. Jesus said unto them, If God were your Father, ye would love me: for I proceeded forth and came from God; neither came I of myself, but he sent me. Why do ye not understand my speech? even because ye cannot hear my word. Ye are of your father the devil, and the lusts of your father ye will do. He was a murderer from the beginning, and abode not in the truth, because there is no truth in him. When he speaketh a lie, he speaketh of his own: for he is a liar, and the father of it. And because I tell you the truth, ye believe me not. Which of you convinceth me of sin? And if I say the truth, why do ye not believe me? He that is of God heareth God's words: ye therefore hear them not, because ye are not of God. (John 8:41–47)

Adam Clarke the commentator sheds light on this passage in a telling way. He cites the old proverb: 'like father, like son'. That is the gist of Jesus' teaching here. When the Jews claim that God is their Father Jesus is ready with His reply. Men who are related to one another show their kinship. When they are father and son they cannot hide it. The marks of the father are on the son, for those who have eyes to see them. The voice of the father sounds through the son, for those who have ears to hear it.

Now Jesus had such eyes and ears. He knew how to account for their unbelief. They were the devil's children; therefore, they could not believe. Their moral kinship with Satan blinded them. 'Ye cannot hear my word,' said Jesus. Why not? Because 'ye are of your father the devil, and the lusts of your father ye will do.' A moral change was needed. Let these men give up wanting to do the lusts of the devil, and the hindrance will be gone. Then all will be well. But that is what they cannot do. They are their father's children.

This comes out clearly in Jesus' words: *'because* I tell you the truth, ye believe me not.' Truth is the one thing they cannot grasp, the one thing foreign to them. They are repelled by it. They are drawn, rather, to lies. It is in their nature. They get it from their father. That is the way they are.

And that is the way we are. Or, at least, that is the way we were before the grace of God came to save us. If we now feel some small love for the truth, we have God to thank. If we have embraced Christ we may be sure it is because God first embraced us. Only those who are 'of God' hear God's words, Jesus tells us. God must work first; then men hear. And the work He must do is far more than conviction of sin or anything else that can happen to an unchanged man. First, men must be 'of God', that is, born again. Then they will hear, and not till then.

6: *New Birth (continued)*

All through this book so far we have been seeking to find light on a question. The question is this: How did it happen that you turned to Christ, that you embraced Him? Now we have the answer. And what an answer it is! God changed you within. That is why you embraced Christ. That is why you believed in Him. And I, like millions before me, have called that change, as the Bible does, a 'new birth', a 'being born again'. Through the rest of the book I will continue to use those terms for the change God has made at the core of our lives. You and I, if we are Christians, have been born again.

We must not think, however, that Scripture always (or even usually) confines itself to the figure of birth to describe this change. Far from it! There is rich variety in God's Word on this theme. We will speak of 'new birth'. But we will add to our understanding of this change the wealth of meaning suggested by other ways of looking at it. I have in mind the following comparisons especially: first, the resurrection of a dead man; second, the healing of a man who is blind. To these we will turn next.

John Murray somewhere makes this point. He tells us that since the Lord Jesus is the brightest and best display of God's character something else surely follows. It is this. The natural man, who hates God, will disclose his own enmity to God most intensely when Christ is plainly set before him. Where God is best revealed, God is most hated.

The Gospel of John confirms this. It is a record of men's hatred towards Jesus. It is also a record of their zeal to kill Him (see, for example, 5:16–20; 7:19; 8:59; 10:30, 31).

At first the passion to kill the Lord was frustrated. His hour had not come – the hour of death, set by His Father. Soon, however, things changed. From God's side the time came near when the Lord Jesus would offer Himself as a sacrifice for sin. That is why He had come to this world. From the human side His enemies' frustration led them to joint action. A meeting of the Jews' ruling council was held. There the high priest called for Jesus' death. John tells us the result. 'Then from that day forth they took counsel together for to put him to death' (John 11:53). And this time, of course, they succeeded.

The thing that interests us here is this. That final meeting, that all-out effort to silence Jesus, was prompted by a resurrection from the dead. Jesus brought Lazarus out of the tomb and back to life. That stupendous act was too much for these men. They could not bear it. It turned them into men more desperate than ever to be rid of Jesus once and for all.

In a way their reaction makes sense. It has a certain twisted logic about it. Jesus' disclosure of God's power in raising Lazarus was so magnificent that it seemed to demand an equally large response. This they gave, in the only way they knew. The law of equal and opposite reaction was at work here. They planned nothing less than the death of God!

Scripture takes it for granted that there can be no greater operation on a man than to raise him from the dead. It is not hard to see why. A dead man cannot co-operate. Neither his heart nor his head nor his hands can contribute one thing to his resurrection. His ears can hear no instructions. His lips can give no consent. If he could do any of these things he would not be dead. How glorious, then, is a resurrection! In launching their final attack on the Son of God Jesus' enemies testified to this fact. They met His great work with an intensity seldom seen, an intense repudiation of who He was and of what He did. This was their way of saying to us, 'How great a thing is a resurrection!'

I wonder if you have seen something else about resurrection. Have you noticed how often God's Word likens what we have been calling 'the new birth' to a resurrection from the dead? I am thinking of such statements as these:

> But God, who is rich in mercy, for his great love wherewith he loved us, even when we were dead in sins, hath quickened us [brought us to life] together with Christ . . . and hath raised us up . . . (Ephesians 2:4–6). And you, being dead in your sins . . . hath he quickened [brought to life] together with him, having forgiven you all trespasses . . . (Colossians 2:13). The hour . . . now is, when the dead shall hear the voice of the Son of God: and they that hear shall live. (John 5:25). We know that we have passed from death unto life, because we love the brethren. (I John 3:14)

What do these statements mean?

I think we can get hold of the meaning by following Paul's line of thought in the Ephesians passage. We will start in chapter one. There Paul tells the Ephesians that he prays for them, and he goes on to list his requests, the things he asks God to do for them. In that list he includes a prayer to this effect: may God open your eyes to grasp the greatness of His power that is at work in believers (v.19). It is, Paul says, the very power that raised Christ from the dead (v.20).

In chapter two Paul makes good his claim. Reflect on this, he tells them. At the outset of your Christian lives nothing short of resurrection power had to come into play. You were dead, weren't you? You will have to admit that (v.1). And what did God do? Why, He raised you from the dead. He brought you to life. He exercised the same power in your case that He put forth in Christ's case. Christ was dead and you Ephesians were dead. But God loved Christ and God loved you. With what result? Christ is alive and you are alive. He raised you as He raised Christ (vv.4-6). That is the power I want you to understand – in all its surpassing greatness and glory!

In a way this book is also a small effort to enter into the spirit of Paul's prayer. For what Paul prayed for the Ephesians he would wish for every believer. He would want us all to have our eyes opened to the greatness of the power of God that brought us to Christ. It is not, of course, that we have had no idea of that power. All along we have known that our new birth was a grand thing. But perhaps we did not know how great a work it was. We were dead; not feeble, not sick, but dead. We were insensible to God. Each of us was Lazarus in the tomb. Then God called us by name. He brought us to life. He brought us up from a grave of unbelief and hatred towards Himself into a new life of faith and love. Our faith was His gift. To God be the glory!

Before we leave this picture of God raising the dead I must make one more point. It is this. Resurrection is God's characteristic work. It is the work He is known by. We know Bill here as a bricklayer. Mary there is a seamstress. They are known by what they do. It is not that they never do anything else. Of course they do. But these are their characteristic works. These are the works they are known by.

So God also has His characteristic work. No doubt, because He is God, He may be characterized by many things. He can do (and does) millions of things by which He might be known if we had eyes to see. That is important to know. We do not want to lose that truth. But along with it we see something else. To judge by Scripture, God likes to be known as the One who gives life, the One who raises the dead.

Through Paul, God the Father calls Himself the God 'who quickens [gives life to] the dead' (Romans 4:17). Elsewhere He taught Paul 'that we should not trust in ourselves, but in God which raiseth the dead' (2 Corinthians 1:9). In neither of these places is the resurrection at the last day especially in view. These are not statements about what God the Father will someday do. Rather, they are in the Bible to tell us what kind of God we have right now.

We find the same sort of thing said about God the Son. In comparing the Lord Jesus with the first man on earth Paul wrote:

> The first man Adam was made a living soul; the last Adam was made a quickening [life-giving] spirit. (1 Corinthians 15:45)

And we must not forget Jesus' own words:

I am the resurrection, and the life: he that believeth in me, though he were dead, yet shall he live: and whosoever liveth and believeth in me shall never die. (John 11:25, 26).

These verses from John are particularly helpful. It is as though you and I spoke to Christ and asked, 'Who are You? How would You characterize Yourself? He replies, 'I am the Resurrection!' 'What does that take in?' we next ask.

'Not just the resurrection in the future,' He replies. 'Living believers were once dead, but I have given them life. In fact, raising the dead is My characteristic work.'

Resurrection is God's characteristic work. There is indeed to be a future resurrection of the bodies of both just and unjust. But God has not been content to wait. Right now He is raising the dead. He did it yesterday; He will do it tomorrow. Father, Son and Spirit (see John 6:63) are at this work continually.

What we sometimes call the new birth may also be called our 'resurrection'. If we are believers in this great God it is not by accident. It is by design. It is because God made up His mind to raise us up, to bring us to life from among the dead. He wanted to be known – in us, and by us – as the One who raises the dead.

Here is another way to view the new birth. We may look at it as the healing of a blind man. Earlier we talked a bit about blindness, but I refrained from saying much about its remedy. The time has come to look beyond the disease to its cure. With that in mind we want to hear some words of Paul:

> But if our gospel be hid, it is hid to them that are lost: in whom the god of this world hath blinded the minds of them which believe not, lest the light of the glorious gospel of Christ, who is the image of God, should shine unto them . . . For God, who commanded the light to shine out of darkness, hath shined in our hearts, to give the light of the knowledge of the glory of God in the face of Jesus Christ. (2 Corinthians 4:3, 4, 6)

Paul's first statement brings together two themes that we are already familiar with. (1) Men are blind, and (2) their blindness means that they are the slaves of Satan (called here 'the god of this world'). That is the condition of all unbelievers. It was Paul's own condition before he knew Christ. He speaks from experience, as well as by inspiration.

But there is more. Paul thinks of the pitch darkness of men's hearts and calls to mind the earth at its creation.

> The earth was without form, and void; and darkness was upon the face of the deep (Genesis 1:2).

Yet God did not leave the earth in that state. He said, 'Let there be light', and by this word He dispelled the darkness.

Now, Paul tells us, God has done the same thing to scatter our darkness. The way to rid a place of darkness is to let the light in. And that is the way God chose to deal with us. God 'shined in our hearts,' says Paul. That is what has made the difference.

Note carefully that it is 'letting the light in' that Paul has in view. When Jesus came, light shone in the world. In some sense, the world was a brighter place just because He came. But that is not Paul's point. Paul's heart was coal-black long after Jesus came into the world. His blindness remained even after he knew about Jesus. It was not until God let the light in that Paul was made new. It was not Paul who let the light in. Paul fought against the light. It was God, who 'shined in our hearts'. The new creation is like the first creation. God speaks, and light appears.

But what is this light that comes to bring men the new birth? Paul does not leave us to guess. He tells us in the latter half of verse 6. The light is knowledge, 'the knowledge of the glory of God in the face of Jesus Christ.' This phrase is so packed with good things that we must look at it more closely.

First, the light is knowledge. Man's blindness and darkness is ignorance, lack of understanding. How shall his blindness be healed? How does one dispel ignorance? By knowledge, of course. Nothing else will do. But what kind of knowledge is needed? Paul says, 'the knowledge of the glory of God.' Here we must stop and weigh his words carefully. For, Paul tell us, not any kind of knowledge of God will do. 'The knowledge of the glory of God' is Paul's phrase. That is the knowledge the new birth brings.

To get what Paul is driving at we need to remember something else he has taught. There is a sense, Paul tells the Romans, in which all men already know God. There are things about God that cannot be hid. Both nature and conscience show us enough of God to bring out our hatred of Him. After all, it would be meaningless to speak of men hating God if they did not know Him in some sense. They might hate the word 'God'. Or they might hate some idea they associated with that word. But all that would not add up to the enmity that the Bible tells us exists between man and God. No, men know God well enough to hate Him.

What men do not know of God is this: they do not know the glory of God. They do not see Him as glorious. Men may see God as terrible. They may be able to say with feeling, 'It is a fearful thing to fall into the hands of the living God' (Hebrews 10:31). But they do not fall before Him in adoring wonder. They do not find that what God is, and what He does, moves them to admiration. They cannot say with conviction, 'O LORD our Lord, how excellent is thy name in all the earth!' (Psalm 8:9).

There is a way, of course, in which the natural man can have a glorious god. He may make up his own. He may create a god who seems glorious to himself. He may even suppose that his god is the God the Scriptures describe. More than likely, his god will be a reflection of the man himself. He may call himself a Christian. But in the true God of the Bible he will find nothing glorious. If he hears the God of the Bible preached he will not admire Him. His enmity to the true God will remain the same so long as he remains a natural man. His need to know 'the glory of God' will remain.

Yet Paul goes further. He tells us that men must receive this knowledge *in the face of Jesus Christ*. What can this mean?

I can answer this question best by asking another. What does Paul mean when he calls Christ 'the image of God'? (2 Corinthians 4:4). Surely he means to tell us this: if we want to know what God is like we must look at the Lord Jesus. Jesus' character is God's character. Jesus' work is God's work. What God is, the Lord Jesus is. And – this is the major point – if God is glorious we may expect to see that glory in the Person ('face') of Christ. Paul saw God's glory there. He urges us to see it there also. For that reason he called the message he preached 'the glorious gospel of Christ'. Or, as others translate it, 'the gospel of the glory of Christ'.

It seems to me that Paul expressed himself here the way he did because of the way he was brought to God. The Book of Acts tells us his story. Briefly, it is this. While Paul was opposing the Light (the Lord Jesus) in every way he could, one day he set out for Damascus to harass the Christians who lived there. Acts describes him as 'breathing out threatenings and slaughter against the disciples of the Lord' (9:1). Certainly he was in no mood to become a Christian. Without warning, however, around noon Paul was startled by a light that surpassed the sun in strength. At the same time the Lord Jesus spoke to him. The effect of these things was twofold. Outwardly he was struck blind. But inwardly a light dawned that was never to go out. The glorious God illuminated Paul's life and Paul's heart. God did it by confronting Paul with Christ. In Christ Paul found Someone to admire and to wonder at. In Christ Paul found God glorious. When, a few days later, his sight was restored he went forth to proclaim Jesus as the Son of God.

Paul sees his experience as a pattern repeated each time God saves a man. God lights up the heart of the sinner as He lit up Paul's heart. God heals the spiritually blind as he healed Paul's sight. God dispels the darkness. He gives understanding. God does all this by showing men his own glory in Jesus Christ. They find God in Christ, and they find Him glorious. Then the sinner goes on his way rejoicing and saying with yet another blind man, 'One thing I know, that, whereas I was blind, now I see!' (John 9:25). To God alone be the glory! Truly, 'the LORD openeth the eyes of the blind' (Psalm 146:8).

The new birth, then, is much more than a new birth. It is life from the dead; it is sight for the blind. I do not know all the other things it may be, but we have seen enough of it to know that God alone could bring a man to the new birth. God alone raises the dead. God alone gives sight to the blind. To speak of man himself doing something towards his own birth is out of the question. That much is clear. Once he is born there is much he can do and must do. But until he is born anew he is in the hands of forces against which he is helpless.

I want to close this chapter by a small bit of verse from Charles Wesley. In thinking on the things we have looked at in this chapter these lines leap out at me. They are from the hymn 'And can it be'. I cannot subscribe to some of Wesley's theology. But, at the same time, I cannot imagine how anyone could better set down the truth about the new birth than that good man has done in these brief lines. See if you do not agree.

> Long my imprison'd spirit lay,
> Fast bound in sin and nature's night:
> Thine eye diffused a quick'ning ray;
> I woke: the dungeon flamed with light!
> My chains fell off, my heart was free,
> I rose, went forth, and followed Thee.

I am tempted to expound these lines as one would a passage of Scripture. The truths we have looked at in this chapter are all there. But I will not. Instead, if you do not see them in Wesley's words, I beg you to read them until you do. And then go on your face before God and thank Him for that 'quick'ning ray'. Thank Him that He ever saved a dead and blind sinner like you. We can never thank Him too much. Too little, indeed, but never too much!

7: *The Father as Source*

Let us see how far we have come. I have tried to show that there is no escape from this fact: faith is a gift from God. That means *your faith* is God's gift to you. And, of course, my own faith is God's gift to me. Wherever there is genuine trust in Jesus Christ, there is God's gift.

Basically I have followed out two lines of thought. First, I have brought out the Bible's own view of man. If we take the Bible at all seriously, I have said, we have man's helplessness and blindness and enmity towards God to face. Man has fallen out with God. Man's bias is away from God. He has no power within himself to put things right. The case is really hopeless from a human point of view. The Bible leaves us no ground at all for expecting the natural man to turn in faith to God or Christ. So, if we find a man with faith – and, thank God, we often do find such a man – we can only conclude that his faith has been given to him. It goes without saying that only God could give such a gift.

Second, I have said that we must let the Bible speak to us about the nature of the new birth. The very name 'new birth' suggests its nature. It is an act of God, purely and simply. Man can no more bring about his new birth than his first birth. Yet, short of this, he will never have faith. His old life is a life of rebellion and unbelief. That will never change until he has new life. And who can bestow new life but God? Or, to change the figure, who but God can take out the heart of stone and replace it with a heart of flesh? Who but God can raise the dead? Who but God can heal the blind? No one, of course; least of all the man or woman who is content to be hard and dead and blind. We shall have to give the glory to God, and we shall rejoice to do so.

Now you will see what I have done. I have pointed out a certain class of Scripture passage; that is, the kind that shows us why faith *must be* a gift from God. What I have not done is this: I have not yet concentrated on those passages that say, more or less directly, that faith *is* a gift. I want to do that next.

You may remember that party spirit had divided the church at Corinth in Greece. One party looked up to Paul as its hero. Another party let its admiration for Apollos separate it from its brethren. Still another party formed around the name of Peter. Each group was in danger of allowing its hero's honour to displace the honour due to Christ. Since there could be no quicker way to destroy the church, Paul rebuked them. He first showed the Corinthians that they were acting like ungodly men in promoting their parties. Then he dealt with their heroes in this way:

> Who then is Paul, and who is Apollos, but ministers by whom ye believed, even as the Lord gave to every man? I have planted, Apollos watered; but God gave the increase. So then neither is he that planteth anything, neither he that watereth; but God that giveth the increase. (1 Corinthians 3:5–7)

Paul gives these Corinthians a large dose of theology

79

to set them right. Their trouble was this. They had too high a view of good men, and too low a view of God. How often the church suffers from this! Since Paul had shared the gospel with some of them, and Apollos had preached when others of them were converted, they were ready to credit the ministers with a power that they did not have. No, no, says Paul! Any success in preaching comes from God. Paul and Apollos are like farmers who plant and water their crops. Their work needs to be done. But as compared to making the crops grow, their work is nothing and they are nothing. Plants spring up everywhere without farmers. But no plant ever yet sprang up without life from God.

So it is with the preaching of the gospel. The preacher aims at success. But he has no power to produce it. The success he seeks is the reception by faith of his message. If his message is met by faith in those who hear, he rejoices. But the whole thing is out of his hands. No amount of argument or eloquence will bring forth faith. The whole issue is in the hands of God. God gives the increase (faith), or withholds it, as it pleases Him. So then, God is everything, His instruments nothing. How foolish to praise the instruments and ignore the hand that wields them, the hand of God!

It is only this kind of imbalance between what God does and what man does that allows Paul to say that ministers are *nothing*. In any kind of joint project that you and I might take up, credit would go to both of us. You might be able to say that your part was a good deal more important than mine. But you could not say that mine was nothing. Or, I might claim to have done 95% of the work, but that would still leave 5% of the credit for you. But Paul does not talk that way. He gives the worker no credit and he gives the hearer no credit. The work of producing faith in the gospel is not 99% God's and 1% man's. Faith is God's gift and His alone. Paul and Apollos are instruments through whom the Corinthians believed. But the faith itself is the work of God. Hear Paul's words once more: 'God gave the increase.' And hear again his astonishing conclusion: 'So then, neither is he that planteth any thing, neither he that watereth; but God that giveth the increase.'

As we have seen, Paul traces faith back to the power of God. God gives faith as He gives life. Turning now to James, we see him tracing faith back to God's choice. Men have faith by God's decision first of all, not by their own.

> Hearken, my beloved brethren, Hath not God chosen the poor of this world [to be] rich in faith, and heirs of the kingdom which he hath promised to them that love him? (James 2:5)

You will notice that I have added the two words 'to be' to the King James Version in order to bring out the sense. In doing this I have followed most of the modern translations. In fact, I believe that all the modern committee versions do this. By 'committee versions' I mean those done by more than a single scholar. My reason is this. As the text stands we might understand it to mean either (1) God chose the poor *to be* rich in faith and heirs of the kingdom, or (2) God chose the poor *who are* rich in faith and heirs of the kingdom. Perhaps either of these translations is correct. The second one, however, is easily misunderstood. We must not make it mean, 'God chose the poor *because* they are rich in faith and heirs of the kingdom.' That would put James at odds with all the rest of Scripture. Surely God does not choose men who are already heirs of the kingdom. That would put the cart before the horse. On whatever basis God chooses, He chooses men *to be* His heirs, not because they are already His heirs.

So, as I have said, all the modern translation committees whose work I have examined have added the words 'to be' to show the sense.

With this in mind let us follow James' argument. The passage (2:1–9) has to do with how we Christians are to treat men who come into the Christian assembly. James notices that well-dressed rich men are often treated with honour, while poor men are slighted. This kind of partiality, he says, has no place among Christians. And he gives his reasons. Verse 5 contains the first one. When any Christian group honours the rich above the poor it acts exactly contrary to its Master. God honours the poor. He does it by making them rich in faith and by making them His heirs. But the church often does the opposite. It gives its gifts of recognition to the rich whom God has chosen to pass over. How much has the church yet to learn of the spirit of its Lord!

We must not suppose, however, that God finds something in poor men to applaud. If He did, He would reward the poor man, of course. And then the poor man's faith and inheritance could be traced up to something in the man himself. Neither his faith nor his inheritance would be a gift in the fullest sense. They would be his wages, a tribute paid to his goodness. One might think that the reward was out of all proportion to the little virtue God observed, whatever that virtue might be. But you could not think of it purely as a gift.

As we have seen earlier, there is nothing in the natural man to reward. There is no goodness in him. God's choice of the poor is God's way of showing that we cannot earn His gifts. God chooses to give His gifts to men who have nothing to offer in exchange. We understand, of course, that the richest man in the world also has nothing to give, but the world does not look at him in that light. The world sees the rich man as a man who can exercise power and wealth to influence God. He can buy God's favour by magnificent acts of charity. He can even pay others to pray for him in this life and after he is dead. A man who does not know where his next meal is coming from cannot do these things. So, naturally, the world honours the rich. In doing that, it misses God's point – the freeness of His grace. God gives to those who have nothing with which to pay. *God makes them rich* by giving them faith. He does this simply, because, as God, He chooses to do so.

Paul teaches us the same truth. I have in mind these words from 1 Corinthians 1:26–29:

> For you see your calling, brethren, how that not many wise men after the flesh, not many mighty, not many noble, are called: but God hath chosen the foolish things of the world to confound the wise; and God hath chosen the weak things of the world to confound the things which are mighty; and base things of the world, and things which are despised, hath God chosen, yea, and things which are not, to bring to nought things that are: that no flesh should glory in his presence.

What kind of men were the believers at Corinth?

Paul says that not many were wise men or mighty men or noblemen. The men and women there who believed in Christ were not from 'the better classes'. Was that an accident? No, says Paul, that is the way God worked it out. God chose people who were not looked up to by the world (vv. 27, 28). He followed up His choice by 'calling' the people whom He had chosen (v. 26).

We want to look closely at the idea of 'calling'. Most of us, I think, are familiar with two kinds of calls. One kind is an invitation. The Lord Jesus seems to have meant this kind of call when he said, 'Many are called, but few are chosen' (Matthew 22:14). That is, many are invited to come to Him, yet relatively few come. This call goes out when we preach the gospel. We invite men to turn to Christ. Some do come, but most do not. But whether successful or not, the gospel call is an invitation to come. The invitation goes out to wise and foolish, rich and poor, without distinction.

There is another kind of call that some of us have had to answer. It is a summons. A summons differs from an invitation. When a county or city sends you a summons it never has R.S.V.P. engraved on it. A summons is an order. It tells you to come to a certain spot on such-and-such a day. It specifies the hour and it has all the authority of the county or city behind it to make sure that you come. God 'calls' men in this way also.

When God calls a man in this sense, however, there is an important difference. It is this. The man cannot flee; he cannot hide; he cannot get away. The trouble with the authority of the city is that it ends at the city limits. A man can get beyond the reach of a summons issued by the city. The authority of the county is likewise limited. It ends at the county line, and a man may get beyond it. But no man can get outside the power of God. Every man, therefore, who is summoned by God in this way answers the call. For that reason 'Those who are called' comes to be another Bible name for Christians. Along with His general invitation to turn to Christ, God issues a summons to some, and they come. They can do nothing else. Paul and James make the same point about these. God calls these from among the poor and insignificant of this world.

I think you will want to see this use of the word 'called' illustrated further. We can start right here in 1 Corinthians 1. Verses 23–24 say:

> We preach Christ crucified, unto the Jews a stumbling-block, and unto the Greeks foolishness; but unto them which are *called*, both Jews and Greeks, Christ the power of God, and the wisdom of God.

Note how Paul divides mankind. There are the Jews. To them Christ is a stumblingblock. There are the Greeks. To them Christ is foolishness. Finally, there are the called. To them Christ is power and wisdom from God. The called, of course, are Christians. The names are synonymous.

The well-known verse, Romans 8:28, is another example of this use of *called*. 'We know,' Paul writes, 'that all things work together for good to them that love God, to them who are the called according to his purpose.' Who are 'the called?' Are they all those who have heard the gospel? Clearly not! The called are those who love God; in other words, the Christians.

This verse also shows the link that the writers of Scripture find between coming to Christ and God's decision that lies behind man's response. The call is said to be according to God's purpose. God laid plans in eternity past to bring men to faith in Christ. And those plans work out. All those called (in this sense) come, as verse 30 goes on to show. ('Whom he called, them he also justified.')

In these verses, then, Paul echoes James' conviction that God has 'chosen the poor of this world [to be] rich in faith' (James 2:5). Paul, too, traces up our faith to God's choice and not our own. We had nothing to pay with. Our works were evil. Yet God

> hath saved us, and called us with an holy calling, not according to our works, but according to his own purpose and grace, which was given us in Christ Jesus before the world began . . . (2 Timothy 1:9)

By changing our hearts God made His call meet with faith on our part. To God be the glory!

In this chapter I have talked about God as the source of faith. When we meet the word 'God' in the New Testament we usually understand that God the Father is meant. In the next chapter I want us to look at texts that show both the Lord Jesus and the Holy Spirit as the source of faith.

Let me close this chapter by pointing out some texts to which you may want to give some further thought. I will discuss these only briefly. Then you can think them over for yourself.

In Acts 18:27 Apollos is said to have helped those who 'had believed through grace'. We meet this phrase in passing. It plays no great part in Luke's story. Yet it shows how men come to faith in Christ and increase in their knowledge of Him. Without mentioning God's name Luke points us to Him, for, of course, the grace is God's grace. God is the source of faith.

I hope you will want to think also on Acts 11:21:

> The hand of the Lord was with them: and a great number believed, and turned unto the Lord.

The scene of this revival was Antioch in Syria. Antioch was the third city of the Roman Empire, and was about to become the starting-point of Christian missions that would reach Rome itself. It was a city of interest to every believer. Notice how Luke accounts for the great work there. He points to the hand of the Lord. The phrase, 'the hand of the Lord', is frequent in the Old Testament. It refers to the power of God. So, Luke tells us, God was powerfully at work. And the result was that a great number believed. Once again faith is traced up to God.

Last of all, let us look at a text that speaks of a good deal more than faith, but certainly includes it. It is 1 Corinthians 4:7.

> For who maketh thee to differ from another? and what hast thou that thou didst not receive? now if thou didst receive it, why dost thou glory, as if thou hadst not received it?

We see Paul here still hammering away at the Corinthians' proud spirit. How can a man, who has received everything he has as a gift, keep on boasting about anything? That is Paul's question. (And it applies as much to us as to them.)

Make no mistake about it, he says. If a Christian man has anything, any good thing at all, he received it. From whom? Paul does not say. He does not need to. The Corinthians, dull as they were, could not miss

Paul's point. Whatever Christian virtue they had they got from God. Or, to borrow the words of another New Testament writer, 'Every good gift and every perfect gift is from above, and cometh down from the Father of lights . . .' (James 1:17). The Bible leaves us in no doubt that that includes faith.

8: *The Son and Spirit as Source*

When we discover that God the Father gives faith we have not finished with the subject. Faith (or something that includes it) is also said to come from the Son. Then again the Holy Spirit is said to produce faith in Jesus as Lord. So here I want to take up the part played by the Son and by the Spirit.

I find John's Gospel to be the grand book of faith. When I first became a Christian I underlined in a pocket Gospel of John all the texts that spoke of believing. That was a great help to me. I came to see that faith in Christ was central to Christianity. All else is related to it. Of course, I had no corner on that truth. But underlining the Gospel underlined it in my mind as well. I trust I will never escape the impact of that fact.

I want us to look particularly at John 17. John 17 has been called the 'High-Priestly Prayer of Christ'. The name is a good one. It looks back to the work of the high priest under Moses' law.

The ancient high priest went into the presence of God with the blood of sacrifice. But, always, he had something else with him. On a breastplate over his heart he had the names of the sons of Israel (see Exodus 28:29). The names and the blood entered God's presence together. The names were on the high priest's heart; the blood was in his hands.

The Lord Jesus was about to offer a bloody sacrifice when He prayed this prayer. He was about to offer up Himself. In a matter of hours He would be in His Father's presence. But just now, at a time when He might understandably forget all others, He has His friends on His heart. He is taking both His blood and the names of His friends into the presence of God.

In praying Jesus says that His Father has granted Him authority over all men. The Father has done this, He says, 'that he should give eternal life to as many as thou hast given him' (v.2). And then Jesus tells His Father what He understands eternal life to be. 'This is life eternal, that they might know thee the only true God, and Jesus Christ whom thou hast sent' (v.3). The gift that Jesus gave was this: the knowledge of God and of Himself.

Now it would be easy to misunderstand this. It would be simple to think along these lines: Jesus came and explained who He was and who the Father was. Then He left it to men to decide whether or not they would believe. I call this a misunderstanding of Jesus' words; I am sure it is. No one, I think, would deny that Jesus explained to men who God was. And, of course, both Jesus' life and words revealed who He Himself was. And certainly He called on men to believe. All that is true. Nevertheless there is much more than that in these words.

You will see my meaning if you remind yourself what Jesus called the knowledge He gave. He called it 'eternal life'. If a man did not possess this knowledge he did not have eternal life. Such a man was lost. But if a man did have this knowledge he had eternal life. Such a man was saved. In other words, there was no middle ground. There were not any men who had this knowledge and were debating what to do with it. There were not any men deciding whether or not to receive it, or to believe it. Either men had it and were saved, or they did not have it and were lost.

You see, then, that Jesus is not simply talking about His public speech. He is praying about opening blind eyes. He is talking about carrying out His commission to free the captives of darkness. That means that the knowledge Jesus gave was knowledge *with faith*. In fact, it may not be too much to say that the knowledge *was* faith. We can look at verse 8 and see how Jesus uses the words 'known' and 'believed' as synonyms. Here are His words:

> They . . . have known surely that I came out from thee, and they have believed that thou didst send me.

It would be hard to find any difference in these two phrases. This statement sounds like a form of Hebrew poetry that deliberately repeats the same idea in different words. Let me show you what I mean.

Hebrew poetry differs from our own. We might say that Hebrew poetry rhymes ideas instead of rhyming words. Often the thoughts in successive lines are identical. Only the words vary. Take Psalm 2:4, for example:

> He that sitteth in the heavens shall laugh, the Lord shall have them in derision.

Both phrases say the same thing. It is not by accident. That was the poet's aim.

A comparison will make clear how much Jesus'

words resemble this. Let me put the Psalmist's words and Jesus' words side by side.

He that sitteth in the heavens shall laugh, The Lord shall have them in derision.	They have known surely that I came out from thee, And they have believed that thou didst send me.

The structure certainly looks the same. Each idea seems neatly repeated. This fact in itself would suggest that both phrases used by the Lord Jesus mean the same thing.

But that is not all. Look with me at verse 25. There Jesus says, 'These have known that thou hast sent me.' This is the same thing He said in part of verse 8. The same, that is, with one point of difference. In verse 25 Jesus says His disciples 'know' what He says they 'believe' in verse 8. Put these two considerations together and you will not have a hard time coming to the same conclusion that I have come to. The two words 'know' and 'believe' mean much the same in this context. Or, to put it another way, in giving knowledge Jesus gives faith.

The same thing is true when Jesus is said to give understanding. In giving understanding Jesus gives faith. 1 John 5:20 says:

> And we know that the Son of God is come, and hath given us an understanding, that we may know him that is true, and we are in him that is true . . .

Here also we might easily misunderstand what John means. We might picture men who have understanding pondering what to do with it. Will they follow the Lord or not? Which way are they to go?

Such a picture would miss the point. In John's view,

those who have understanding are Christians. They are not debating about Christianity. They are 'in him that is true'. That is, they belong to God. This is a gift from the Lord Jesus.

I think I can make this clearer by taking a closer look at the word 'understanding'. Our English word 'understanding' is used for two very different ideas. We may say, for example, 'My understanding of the matter is this: George got to the house before Bill.' We mean, these are the facts as I see them. 'Understanding' in this case means 'information'. Now, of course, if the understanding Jesus brought was mere information, then a man might have it and yet not be a Christian.

That, however, is not the meaning of the Greek word John uses. We must not take it that way. Instead, the Greek word matches our English word when we use it another way. Note its use in this sentence: 'James is a man of understanding.' Here is a quite different idea. This does not tell us how much information James has. It tells us, rather, that James has ability, insight, or a disposition to learn. And that catches the force of John's word in Greek. Jesus gives us the disposition to know God.

You will see at once what this means. The whole problem with us before we were brought to Christ was this. We had no disposition to know God. We were biased against Him. That made us unteachable. Had that not been the case we would have put our faith in God from the moment we first heard of Him. That was our great handicap. Now Jesus has removed it. That is why we are Christians. Whoever receives this understanding comes to know God. That is just another way of saying that the understanding Jesus gives brings faith with it. Or you may say that this understanding produces faith. No matter how you put it the truth remains: Jesus' gift makes faith both possible and certain.

We turn now to consider the Holy Spirit as the source of Faith. Is it true that the Father and the Son give faith? Then it is no less true that the Holy Spirit gives faith as well. We must take up this point next.

Do you remember Paul's description of the way to be saved in Romans 10:9? He says:

> If thou shalt confess with thy mouth the Lord Jesus, and shalt believe in thine heart that God hath raised him from the dead, thou shalt be saved.

Now let me ask a question. Which of these two things is easier? Is it easier to say, 'Jesus is Lord'? Or, is it easier to believe in your heart that God raised Him from the dead? Well, we have a proverb that seems to cover cases like this. It says, Talk is cheap. Saying words, even religious words, costs us nothing. Religion is very much with us, and so much of it seems to consist in talk. Surely it is easier to talk than to believe.

Now Paul was no fool. More than most men, I suppose, he had been exposed to religious talk. It may come as a surprise to us, then, to hear something else Paul had to say. In addition to telling us that we must confess Jesus as Lord, he says this: 'No man can say that Jesus is the Lord, but by the Holy Ghost' (1 Corinthians 12:3). He seems to be saying that what we took to be easy is well-nigh impossible. What can he mean?

Of course it is true that no man can say *anything at all* unless God sustains his life. We are not independent beings. We have not been wound up to go along our way without any further attention from God. Quite the opposite! We depend on God for every breath. We lean on Him for every heart-beat. We must never lose sight of that.

But that is not what Paul has in mind here. In that sense every man speaks by the Spirit of God. In that sense there is no other way to speak; there could be no other way. But in the same verse Paul mentions men who do not speak by God's Spirit. Here are his words: 'No man speaking by the Spirit of God calleth Jesus accursed.' So Paul has something else in view when he talks of men speaking by the Spirit of God. What does he mean?

Paul cannot mean that no unconverted man can pronounce these words, 'Jesus is the Lord.' That would not be true. Any man who reads this passage aloud will say, 'Jesus is the Lord.' It will make no difference whether he is a Christian or not. In fact, an unbeliever, skilled in reading, may say these words more distinctly and more attractively than I can say them. Paul's point must lie elsewhere.

Paul means that no one can say these words with the deep-rooted conviction that we call 'Christian faith' except by the Spirit of God. The Spirit is responsible for a man's conviction that Jesus is the Lord. When a believer says, 'Jesus is the Lord', his words reflect the assurance put in his heart by the Holy Spirit. The believer illustrates the truth Jesus taught: 'Out of the abundance of the heart the mouth speaketh' (Matthew 12:34). The heart overflows with this confession: 'Jesus is the Lord!'

If a man says from the heart, 'Jesus is accursed,' we are sure that the Spirit has not been at work in him. His unbelief comes from elsewhere. But what if a man says from the heart, 'Jesus is the Lord'? That man, we may be sure, shows the work of the Spirit in his heart. That man has faith as a gift from the Spirit.

I will come back to the work of the Spirit in a moment, but this would seem to be a good time to make another point. It is this. Paul is not the only one in the New Testament who traces confessions of faith up to God. A marked example is Jesus' comment on Peter's confession in Matthew 16. There Jesus speaks first. He asks His disciples a question:

> Whom say ye that I am? And Simon Peter answered and said, Thou art the Christ, the Son of the living God.
> And Jesus answered and said unto him, Blessed art thou, Simon Bar-jona: for flesh and blood hath not revealed it unto thee, but my Father which is in heaven. (Matthew 16:15-17)

How did Peter come to make this grand confession? Jesus has two answers to that question. First, it was not by 'flesh and blood'. That is, according to a common Jewish way of speaking, it was not by frail human power. We must look beyond Peter's own abilities to understand how he arrived at this true view of Jesus. Second, it was a revelation. God the Father revealed this truth to Peter. What Peter could not grasp as a mere man, God gave to him. It was Peter's confession of faith, but, behind and beyond that, it was a gift from God.

But let us return to the work of the Spirit. We have not yet looked at a very important text on the subject of His work in bringing men to Christ. It occurs in Jesus' conversation with Nicodemus. I want to take that up next. Jesus is speaking:

Verily, verily, I say unto thee, Except a man be born of

water and of the Spirit, he cannot enter into the kingdom
of God. That which is born of the flesh is flesh; and that
which is born of the Spirit is spirit. Marvel not that I said
unto thee, Ye must be born again. The wind bloweth
where it listeth [wants to], and thou hearest the sound
thereof, but canst not tell whence it cometh, and whither
it goeth: so is every one that is born of the Spirit. (John
3:5–8)

This passage is full of good things. But, to stay on the
subject, we will confine ourselves to the ideas connected
with the phrase, 'born of the Spirit'.

You will see at once that there is a contrast here. It
is found in the phrases, 'born of the flesh', and 'born
of the Spirit'. Two births are in view, and each is
described by its source. We are told that one birth is a
product of the flesh; the other is a product of the Spirit.
One birth comes to every man; the other, only to some.
But I have not yet touched the main difference. It lies
here. One birth, within certain limits, is under the
control of the will of man. Men and women can choose
to conceive and bear children of the flesh. Since they
are flesh, they may choose to produce flesh. Their
power of choice is not absolute. It may be frustrated.
Yet it is real. But this other birth, this birth by the
Spirit, is quite different. To describe it, Jesus adopts
an illustration that leaves man passive.

Being born of the Spirit, Jesus says, is like being
acted upon by the wind. The wind blows where it
wants to. You can see its effects, but you cannot
control it. You may wish it to blow here or there, but
your wish will not change the course of the wind. It
does as it pleases. So, too, the Spirit acts on men as He
pleases. And we know His work by its effects. He
brings this man to birth, to new life, while passing that

man by. This is the freedom of the Spirit. We can give no account of it beyond saying that it pleases Him. He delights in creating men and women who are born, as John tells us, 'not of blood, nor of the will of the flesh, nor of the will of man, but of God'. (John 1:13)

Now where does faith fit into this picture? Let me repeat what I said earlier, and then I will add just a word more.

'Repentance and faith, then, are signs that the new heart is there. They are birth cries of the new creature . . . God makes a new man who delights in exercising faith towards God. The new man's faith is really his own. It flows out of his new life. It is he, not God, who believes. Yet the faith is from God, a gift, pure and simple. In giving the new heart God gives the faith.'

My additional word is this. We have now gone a step further. We see that the Lord Jesus pointed out the Holy Spirit as the special author of the new birth. Men 'born of God' are 'born of the Spirit'. So we cannot escape a further conclusion. The Holy Spirit, in giving life, makes it certain that faith will follow. And that is just another way of saying that faith is a gift from the Spirit of God.

9: *Faith Further Defined*

No one who has come with me this far can be in doubt about my central point. It is this: faith – that faith which turns to and embraces Christ – is the gift of God. I have not offered this as my opinion, though I certainly believe it. I have said, rather, that the Scripture forces this conclusion. It does so in two ways. First, it shows us a natural man who is not able to believe. Second, it teaches us that Father, Son, and Holy Spirit do things to some men – momentous things – that make certain that faith will follow. These momentous acts of God are summed up in the phrase, 'the new birth'. By this 'birth' men are brought to faith. As men are born of God they exercise faith as truly and naturally as a new-born baby breathes.

It is time, now, to take a closer look at faith. We know, of course, that men do not become Christians by learning to define faith. But it seems silly to talk about the importance of faith if we have no wish to know as much about it as we can. Faith links us to God. That is no small work. It beckons to us to give it closer attention. That is what we must do next.

First, I want to talk a bit about the way the man in the street uses the word 'faith' in the ordinary ups and downs of life. 'Faith' is a common word. Often it has nothing to do with religion. We hear things like this:

'I have no faith in the man.' Or this: 'You can put your faith in this medicine.' Or this: 'He has no faith in the newspapers.' Such things may be heard any day in the week. The question is: what do these things mean? What is the common idea that lies behind these uses of 'faith'?

The common idea is this. The things we express faith in (or lack of faith in) are things that seem to claim, in one way or another, to be trustworthy. They call on us to trust them, to rely on them. If a man says to a child, 'I will buy you some ice-cream,' he invites the child to trust him to do so. He has said, 'Trust me.' And he has told the child what to rely on him for.

The same holds true for *things* like medicines and newspapers. They too invite our trust. A medicine cannot speak, of course. But some person who can speak (or write) will put forth claims for it. It may be the manufacturer. In that case we find the claims on the box or on the label. It may be a friend who puts forth the claims. In that case he tells us how this drug may be relied on to relieve arthritis or headache or a persistent cough, or all of these and more! In either case the claims come with the medicine and invite our trust. In the same way the newspaper claims to tell us the truth about our town and our world. It too says, 'Believe me. I can be relied on. I am trustworthy.'

You will see at once that there are several possible ways to respond to claims like these. To make them more real, let's suppose that you and I are children. Someone comes along and offers to buy us some ice-cream. Let me make a list of the things we might do.

1. We might wonder what is meant. We might wonder, for example, what ice-cream is.

2. We might disbelieve the offer.

3. We might be indifferent. We might like the toys we are playing with better than the thought of ice-cream.

4. We might rely on the offer and expect the ice-cream. (I can taste it now!)

Now I said I was making a list 'of things we might do'. This is what I have done. But notice that the list is made up of mental responses. Someone looking at us might not see us *do* anything at the moment when the offer to buy us some ice-cream is made. Keep in mind that we are dealing with mental processes. This will become most important as we proceed.

But back to our list! In looking it over I think we see the things involved in 'faith', as the word is commonly used. First, there is *understanding*. We need to know what ice-cream is. Second, there is *belief*. We agree that the man is really telling the truth. That is, we believe he is willing and able to buy us ice-cream. Third, there is *trust*. We rely on the promise and expect the ice-cream. When these three things come together we are said to have faith.

Before we go on let me clear up one point. I can imagine one of you asking me why I included understanding and belief in faith. After all, you might say, trust, all by itself, is faith. If we trust a promise we have faith in it. If we have faith in a promise we trust it – and that's that!

You are right, of course, if you mean it in the right way. Trust *is* the thing we are after. We might call it faith and leave it at that. There is a danger here, however, that I want us to avoid. If we are not careful we may suppose that trust can exist without understanding and belief. That would be a great mistake. Yet every once in a while we meet people who seem to have just that idea. Trust, for them, is 'a leap in the dark'. What they mean, I think, is this. They have heard that such-and-such a thing is true and they hope that it is. So they will act as though it were true.

For instance, they may have heard a rumour that a sack of gold is being given to everyone who shows up between 8 a.m. and 9 a.m. at 220 Main Street. They are excited. It probably isn't true, but who can tell? 'We're going to have faith that it's true,' they say. So off they go, hoping to get their fortune. They want it to be true, and we wish them well. But their attitude is not 'trust'; it is 'hope', a flimsy hope, at that. It is indeed a leap in the dark.

Yet even in this illustration there is understanding. The vain hope of getting the sack of gold was aroused by knowing what gold is. How many people, do you suppose, would have shown up for a sack of lubulak? (Do not reach for your dictionary. I made the word up!) Not many, I feel sure. You will see, then, that without both understanding and belief there can be no trust. Once we have that clear we may call the trust 'faith'. But we must not forget that where faith is, there also are understanding and belief.

Now that we have the ideas that lie behind the word 'faith' we can take a further step. We are ready to take up the case of faith *in a person*. If faith in a statement or promise is understanding, believing, and trusting the statement or promise, what is faith in a person? Please note that we are still looking at 'faith' as it is commonly used. We have not yet come to Christian faith. Discussing faith in a person, however, will bring us closer to that goal.

It is not unusual for people to think that faith in a

person and faith in a statement are very different things. But then, they are often hard-pressed to point out the difference. One man may explain it in terms of depth. 'I feel way down inside that I would place my life in his hands.' Another may draw on a contrast to make us see what he means. 'You use your head when you trust a statement. When you trust a person you use your heart.' What do these remarks have in common? The idea seems to be this. There is an emotional involvement in trusting a person that is missing when we trust a statement or promise. But is that so?

Keep in mind that when you trust a statement you are trusting a person. Someone made the statement. You trust *him*. Someone spoke the promise or wrote it down. You rely on *him*. Is there really a difference here? Suppose my friend Harry tells me he will pick me up in his car and take me to dinner. If I understand what he says, and if I want to go, what will I do? Will I rely on his statement? Or, will I trust him? They come to the same thing, do they not?

But, still, the suspicion remains: there is a difference. Trusting a person and trusting a statement are not the same thing. Let us see if we can pinpoint the difference.

First, it would be more accurate to say there *may be* a difference. Relying on Harry to pick me up and trusting Harry's promise *are* the same thing. Either is faith. So far there is no difference. What makes them the same is this: both focus on a single event. The man and his promise are both being counted on to do just one thing, to pick me up and take me to dinner.

But suppose we hear a man say, 'I trust my wife.' Is it likely that he has just one event or occasion in mind when he says that? No, it is more likely that he means that he trusts her on all occasions. When we want to single out one act we usually say things differently. We say, 'I trust Michael *to* . . .' Then we fill out the sentence with the one act we have in mind. 'I trust Michael to put out the garbage.' 'I trust Michael to cook the pot roast.' 'I trust Michael to feed the cat.' If we say, 'I trust Michael,' without any addition, we often mean something more. That 'something more' is what we call *faith in a person.*

Let me further illustrate what I mean. If you are like I am, you are sometimes caught without a means of telling the time. Perhaps you have done what I have done. I have said to some stranger, 'Pardon me. Would you please tell me what time it is?'

As far as I can recall I have always received a courteous answer to my question. And I have usually learned the time. Now suppose that, a moment after I said my 'thank you' and went on my way, I ran into a friend who had watched what took place. And suppose he said, 'You don't trust that fellow, do you?' What would I answer?

My answer would depend on what I thought my friend meant. If I took him to mean, 'You don't trust a stranger to tell you the time, do you?' my answer would be easy. 'Yes,' I would say, 'I've done it lots of times. Why not? It always works for me.'

I could understand my friend in another way, however. He might mean, 'You wouldn't trust that fellow on any and every occasion, would you?' In that case I would reply, 'No. Of course not. I don't even know the man. But that doesn't keep me from asking him the time.' The fact is, we often trust people to do this or that for us whom we do not trust in any extensive way. I may know that a certain businessman does not carry on his business in an honest manner. That does not keep me from trusting him to tell me what day of the week it is, or how far it is to the next town. But, still, I could not be said to have faith in his person. That requires something more.

What, then, is faith in a person? How does it differ from faith in a statement? Faith in a person turns out to be, not something different from faith in a statement, but the same thing on a much wider scale. *Faith in a person is a habitual reliance on what that person says.* Who are the persons in whom I have faith? They are the men and women whom I trust in their statements and claims generally.

This is not a question of feeling. Faith in a person is no more emotional than faith in a promise. Either may produce enormous emotion. But neither *is* emotion. Both are primarily mental acts.

It is likely that trust in a dear friend will produce what I might call a quiet emotion. On the other hand, faith in the statement 'Your uncle has just left you two million dollars!' will probably give birth to boisterous feelings, better imagined than described. In neither case, however, is the trust the same as the feeling. The trust gives rise to the feeling. And the emotion created by a simple statement can be as intense, or more so, than the feelings aroused by trust in a friend.

In fact, I must go a step further. I must say that feelings produced by isolated statements are almost bound to be more intense than those aroused by trust in a friend. We saw above that faith in a person is a habitual reliance on what that person says. I might have called it a settled attitude of reliance. The phrase, 'settled attitude', suggests something that goes on and on. And that is precisely what faith in a person does;

it goes on and on. It relies on that person's statements and claims, and it does so repeatedly.

But intense emotion is not like that at all. It thrives on the sudden, the unexpected. Nothing kills intense emotion like repetition. That is why it is so hard to recapture an old thrill. The more intense the emotion is, the shorter it will last. And the harder it will be to get it back. This means that if I insist on measuring my faith by the depth of my feelings I will soon be alarmed. As time wears on my feelings will quieten down. They can do nothing else. If emotion, then, is the yardstick that I put up against my faith I may well wonder if my faith is not decaying instead of growing stronger.

We see this in marriage. A satisfying marriage is one in which trust grows as years pass. But do the intense emotions that the couple knew on their wedding day grow? No, they do not. And it is a good thing. If they did, the darlings would soon be drones on society. Human nature being what it presently is – I do not say how it will be in eternity – exquisite delights make us useless for anything except enjoying exquisite delights!

It is time to ask the question, 'How do we come to faith in a person?' How is it that Michael trusts Mary? (Ordinarily he seems to be such a level-headed boy!) Why do you trust the people you trust? This question will take up the rest of the chapter. Earlier we saw that faith in a statement requires understanding and belief. The same is true for faith in a person. We will look at each in turn, to see how lack of them makes faith impossible.

Take understanding first. Whatever hinders my understanding another man hinders my faith in him.

Think, for instance, of the language barrier. If he speaks Chinese and I speak English, faith will come very hard. In most cases it will not come at all without a third party to help us. To arrive at mutual faith we will need a go-between to interpret our words to each other. Failing that, faith is not impossible, but neither is it likely. Any barrier to understanding is a barrier to faith also.

The same is true of belief. Anything that hinders me from believing what a man says will keep me from relying on him. If I cannot 'believe' Harry, I cannot 'believe in' Harry. That may not keep me from acting as though I trust him. I may take my chances with Harry, but my settled attitude will not be trust or faith in his person. It will be something less.

But now let us suppose that both understanding and belief are present. I understand Harry and I believe him. How do these things pass into faith? What leads me to rely on him?

Let us return to Harry's offer to pick me up in his car and take me out to dinner. Back there I asked, 'If I understand what he says, and if I want to go, what will I do?' In asking that question I brought in something we have not yet discussed. I put in the phrase, 'If I want to go.' If Harry says he will pick me up I believe him. I take it that he is willing and able to do so. Yet it may be that I will not depend on him, or rely on him, or trust him to do so. Why not? *I may not want to go*. Belief passes into faith when I want what Harry offers, and not till then. If I have no desire to go, I will not depend on Harry to take me.

Let me tell you a story. A Boy Scout leader was checking up on three of his boys. 'Well, my lads,' he asked, 'have you done your good deed for the day?'

'Yes, sir!' they answered in chorus.

'And what was it you did, boys?'

'We helped an old lady across the street,' they replied.

The Scoutmaster was impressed, but he had a question. 'Why did it take three of you to help her?'

'Because,' they said in unison, 'she didn't want to go!'

And that is what faith comes down to. I do not have faith if 'I don't want to go.' Could the old lady in the story be said to have had faith in the boys? She had evidence: they were willing and able to take her across the street. No doubt about that! But we would not say that she depended on them, or relied on them, or trusted them, would we? Surely not! What, then, was missing? She had no *desire* to trust them – and so, she did not do so.

Early in this book I asked why one man turns to Christ and another does not. Here are my words.

'What does Jones have that Smith lacks? The obvious answer to the question . . . is, in a word, *inclination*. Or, to use a simpler word, *desire*. Jones *desires* Christ; Smith does not. Jones *is inclined* to turn to Christ; Smith is not.'

The case of trusting Christ will turn out to be typical of all cases of faith in a person. Let us see how that is true.

If what a man is, or what he offers to do, does not appeal to me, I will not rely on him. In every case in which I rely on a person two things meet. First, there is the evidence that he is trustworthy. (This evidence will have to seem adequate to me.) But that is not all. Second, there is also in me an inclination or desire to trust him. I may admit that he is trustworthy without committing myself to him.

On the other hand, if I believe a single promise a man makes, and if I depend on him to carry it out, so far I have faith. I trust him to do such-and-such a thing for me. Beyond that, if I believe his many promises and statements and claims about himself, the door is open to me to have faith in his person. I may rely on all that he says that affects me. Then I will say more than 'I trust Harry to . . .' I will say simply, 'I trust Harry.'

And if I must know – though it may be none of my business – why Michael trusts Mary, it will come to the same thing. In his eyes she is trustworthy. He thinks he sees the evidence that it is so. And not only that, he wants her. His desire, his inclination is towards Mary. Both ingredients are there: trustworthiness (as he sees it), and inclination. Where these two meet, there we have the answer to the question, 'How do we come to faith in a person?'

10: *A Biblical Faith*

You will see at once what I hope to do next. In the last chapter we looked at the way the word 'faith' is used in everyday life. Now I want us to connect that ordinary use with Christian faith, faith in God and Christ. The last chapter laid the groundwork for us to get hold of Biblical faith. That 'getting hold' is what we must do now.

The phrase 'Biblical faith' may have two meanings. It may mean, first, the kind of faith commended in the Bible. A man may be said to have Biblical faith if he has the kind of faith celebrated, for instance, in Hebrews 11. All Christians would agree that that kind of faith – whatever it may be – is desirable. I need not labour that point.

'Biblical faith' may also mean believing the Bible itself. It will be one aim of this chapter to examine Biblical faith in this sense. I have an important reason for doing so. There are an increasing number of voices saying things like this: 'What we need is faith in God, not faith in a book.' Or this: 'Christian faith is faith in a living God, not faith in a dead writing.' If we have not yet heard these things, we may expect to do so. And that brings us to ask: How shall we react to statements like these? Where will these voices take us if we follow them? Is there some truth in what is being said? And, if so, how can we take it in without being led astray?

Let us try to sort out the truth and the error. Where is the truth in the above statements? In each case it is in the first half of the sentence. This is true: 'What we need is faith in God.' This too is true: 'Christian faith is faith in a living God.' No responsible Christian could say less, could he? Faith in the Father and in the Son and in the Holy Spirit *as Persons* is what we are after. Nothing less will suffice. We may put this another way. We may say that the Bible is not an end in itself. No, it is a means to an end. God has given it to us so that, whether read or preached to us, we may be led to put our trust in Him.

There is a further danger, however, in the earlier statements. It lies in those contrasts, 'faith in God, *not* faith in a book', and 'faith in a living person, *not* faith in a dead writing'. Is it really one or the other? Is it really 'either – or'? Why can't it be 'both – and'?

Let me illustrate. Years ago I read something that lodged in my mind, though I doubt that I understood it then. A writer gave it as his view: 'You are more likely to be right in what you affirm than in what you deny.' Well, I suppose that at the time I could not have taken that in at all. If A is true, then B is false, and that is the end of it – that was most likely my attitude at the time. Why would anyone think differently?

But over the years I have changed. The writer was right. What he said amounts to this: the truth is apt to be larger than I take it to be at first glance. If I get hold of part of it I run the danger of taking that part for the whole. I am too much like the blind men who went to 'see' the elephant. When one blind man got hold of the elephant's tail he knew what an elephant was like. 'An elephant,' he said, 'is like a rope.' He was contradicted, however, by his friend who had hold of a leg. 'Not at all,' he replied. 'An elephant is like a tree.' It is still true, of course, that in some cases if A is true, B is false. There are lots of blacks and whites left in the world. But not in as many cases as I once thought.

Let us see how this bears on the Bible. Is there a necessary contrast between a living person and a dead writing? A man might think so if he simply paid attention to the words 'living' and 'dead'. They are loaded emotionally. If one thing is 'living' and another is 'dead', it is not hard to feel a preference for the living thing, whatever it may be. Bringing in such words, however, prejudices the case. They divert our minds from the thing we need to focus on. In this case that thing is the relation of a person to his words.

A few minutes ago my phone rang. It was my friend, Norm, calling. I could not see him, of course, as he spoke. Our only connection was words. He spoke to me. Then I spoke to him. In a short time we worked out a luncheon date. Then we said our good-byes. Now let me ask a question. Would it be fair to say that I was in touch with Norm for those few minutes? Can you imagine someone saying, 'No, you were not. You were only in touch with his words'?

If someone did say that, I would take it as a joke. The reason is this. I am never in closer contact with a person than when I hear his words, *if* his words really represent his thoughts. I add the 'if' because, of course, a man may lie to me. He may hide himself behind false words. But when he tells me the truth, he exposes his person. In conveying his words to me he conveys himself.

Now, what do we find when we turn to the Bible? We find a book that professes to be the word of God. (See Appendix.) When I read the assertions of the Bible I read the word of God. 'Thus saith the Lord' is a common formula. Here, I am told, is truth. I may, of course, reject Scripture. I may say that the Bible claims too much for itself. I may go on my way and forget it, without further ado. I may choose to attack the Scriptures. There are many stances I may take, short of accepting the Bible's own estimate of itself.

But what if I, as a Christian, accept the Bible for what it professes to be? What then? Why, then, I must treat its statements as I treat my friend Norm's statements. I must see them as true words that bring me into close contact with their Author. I must see them, not as a barrier but, as a bridge. I must not pit the word against the Author. In receiving the one I receive the other.

I suppose, however, that someone will think that I have still missed the point. 'The purpose,' he will say, 'of using the word "dead" of the Scriptures is to remind me how out of date they are. They were for another people in another age. Can't you see that?' And for good measure he might add, 'After all, you heard your friend Norm speaking. That's a far cry from reading his words 2000 years later.' Much more, of course, could be said along the same lines.

Nevertheless, the Bible stands as God's word to us. I say that for this reason. The question is not how long ago words were spoken, but whether they still convey the mind of their author. This is true of your words and my words and Norm's words and God's words. I have not yet had my luncheon date with Norm, but his word will stand until that day rolls around. Of course, since he is a mere man, something may hinder him from keeping our engagement. Or, something may stand in my way. Nothing, however, will hinder God from keeping His word. His word cannot be made obsolete. ('Obsolete', I take it, is what 'dead' means in a context like this.)

In fact, the Bible met this objection long before it was raised by modern man. You may see this by comparing the following verses. They tell us to what extent God and Christ retain their intentions towards us and towards this world (Jesus is the speaker in the first verse).

> Heaven and earth shall pass away, but my words shall not pass away. (Matthew 24:35)
> Jesus Christ the same yesterday, and today, and for ever. (Hebrews 13:8)

You will note, also, that the one verse explains the other. It is the unchanging character of God and of Christ – what theologians call their 'immutability' – that explains why their words keep on binding us and encouraging us.

Now, since the Bible conveys the mind of God to us, something else is true. It is this. The Bible gives us just what we need to come to faith in God and in Christ. It brings us their statements, their promises. And what good will that do? To get at the answer, let me quote from my last chapter:

'What, then, is faith in a person? How does it differ from faith in a statement? Faith in a person turns out to be, not something different from faith in a statement, but the same thing on a much wider scale. *Faith in a person is a habitual reliance on what that person says.* Who are the persons in whom I have faith? They are the men and women whom I trust in their statements and claims generally.'

So, if I am to have faith in God and in Christ, I must know their statements and claims. No wonder the Scripture speaks of faith coming by hearing the word concerning God and Christ! And that is just what the Bible provides.

I think I hear someone say, however, 'It is the great acts of God that produce faith. We need to concentrate on them. Things like His creation, His delivering Israel from Egypt, and especially His mighty works in Christ – these inspire faith.' And so they do. But what happens when we ask *why* they do so? The answer brings us right back to the statements and claims of the Bible.

I am not thinking here of the obvious fact that we would know nothing of these 'great acts' if we did not have our Bibles. That is true, however, and must not be overlooked. But there is much more than that to be said.

The great acts of God inspire faith because they are explained to us in God's word. We are helped to understand them. And the help is indispensable. Take the death of Christ, for instance. Is it a great act or not? What shall we make of it? Is it a martyr's death? Is it a needless tragedy? Or – can it be a triumph? Who can tell? The Bible tells, of course, as it makes its statements and claims about Christ and His work.

So we need statements and claims. We need interpretation. I have sometimes thought that God gave the Old Testament Book of Job to show us our need for interpretation. Think of Job's sufferings. Try to put yourself in Job's place. Job has no clue to why these things are happening to him. He can make no sense of them at all. He cannot interpret them.

But the reader is not in the dark. In the first two chapters God draws back the curtain for us. He interprets what is about to happen. Read those chapters first and you have an immense advantage over Job. Job feels the acts of God and Satan. He knows those acts in a way the reader cannot know them. Yet that adds to his misery. Without interpretation Job's sufferings are meaningless. They are meaningless to Job, and they are meaningless to us. They would not and could not inspire faith.

You will see, then, why God has given us His word. His word supplies what we must have to come to faith in Himself. His word is not an end in itself. But it is a necessary means, fitted to lead us to faith in Himself. A Biblical faith, therefore, includes believing in the Bible.

I want us to turn now to the other meaning of Biblical faith. The faith the Bible commends to us is faith in God and in Christ. It urges us to believe in God. It exhorts us to believe in Christ. We must get a grasp of what these things mean. To do that I have chosen to focus on faith in Christ. My reason is this: faith in Christ includes faith in God. We see God in Christ. Old Testament saints believed in God as He was revealed to them. New Testament saints do the same. Our highest revelation of God is in the Lord Jesus. In Paul's phrase, we see 'the glory of God in the face of Jesus Christ' (2 Corinthians 4:6).

So we come to the Bible's claims for Jesus Christ. You will notice that I have already jumped ahead and made an enormous claim for Him in the last paragraph.

One simply must do this if one is to speak of Christ in Biblical terms. I started with the 'glory of God in the face of Jesus Christ'. From there it is but a short step to say with John, 'The Word was God' (John 1:1). ('The Word' is John's name for the Son of God in chapter one of his Gospel.) Jesus Christ was God in the flesh. That is the first statement, the first claim. Could any claim be higher?

But there is more. We find it written, 'Christ Jesus came into the world to save sinners' (1 Timothy 1:15). That too is a great claim, as it is a great work.

Let me add one more. Jesus said, 'No man cometh unto the Father, but by me' (John 14:6). After His resurrection His followers echoed this:

> Neither is there salvation in any other: for there is none other name under heaven given among men, whereby we must be saved.' (Acts 4:12)

That too is a great claim.

Let me sum up the claims the Bible makes for Christ in the verses quoted above. I will put them in one sentence. *Jesus Christ, who is God in the flesh, has come into the world to save sinful men who cannot be saved apart from Him.* Now faith started by coming to terms with these claims. You and I asked ourselves, 'What do I think of this statement, this proposition?' To be more precise, we said:

1. What do these claims mean?
2. Are these claims true?

In fact, we could not avoid asking these questions if we were at all interested.

Now I must guard myself against misunderstanding. I do not mean, of course, that we really spoke these words to ourselves. I did not say, 'What does this mean? Is it true?' Nor, probably, did you. Nevertheless, our mental processes were like these questions. Our ears pricked up when we heard of Christ, to catch *the meaning and likelihood of what we heard*. To be sure, we started our questions at the level of our prior understanding. If you and I, for instance, already knew that 'flesh' here meant human nature – if once and for all that question had been answered for us – we did not ask it again. We went on.

Let us look at this summary sentence again: *Jesus Christ, who is God in the flesh, has come into the world to save sinful men who cannot be saved apart from Him*. Do I understand what this means? Do I believe it? A Christian understands what is said here – not exhaustively, but to some degree – and he believes it to be true. He does not know everything about the Person and work of Christ, but he knows something of the claim made here. His mind has been at work on these facts. And his mind has yielded to them. They are true.

I must not hurry over this too quickly, as though it were the easiest thing in the world. It is not. Believing the truth about Jesus brings us into enormous difficulty when we compare it to believing the truth about other men. The difficulty is this. To have faith in an ordinary person there must be a certain modesty about his claims. He must not claim too much. Yet Jesus freely breaks this rule. And such writers as Paul and John heartily follow His example. No honour is left to be claimed for Jesus that they do not give Him. When you have said, 'Jesus is God', you have said it all.

How have Christians dared to go so far? There are two answers to this question. One has to do with the way God first made man. The other has to do with the way God has made us over again. We might call the one 'the natural answer'. We might call the other 'the supernatural answer'.

The *natural answer* is this. God has made us with a large capacity to believe, to exercise faith. In a sense, we are all looking for an object big enough to match our capacity to believe. That object, though one may not know it, is God in Christ. Augustine's well-known thought remains true: God has made us for Himself, and our hearts are restless until they rest in Him. God is to be found in Jesus Christ. Such is the witness of Scripture. Christians have dared to follow the Scripture's lead. They have dared to say, 'Jesus is God. Here at last is an object to fill all my vision. Christ will call forth all my faith.' There is a natural correspondence here between my capacity for believing and the greatness of the One in whom I believe.

But the natural answer is not enough. It will not stand alone for two reasons. First, it looks a bit too much like wish fulfilment. Here I am, a man with a need to believe in something – something big. I hear about God and Jesus Christ His Son. They seem to meet my need, and presto, I am a believer. It is all so natural to think in this way. 'Ho hum,' the sceptics would be bound to say, 'the wish is father to the thought. So much for his faith!' If the natural answer were all, who would blame them?

Second, the natural answer is not enough, because of the hatred of the natural man towards God. It is true that man seeks a grander object to believe in than he can find outside of God and Christ. But that is not the whole truth. Something else must be said. It is this. The one object that can satisfy him is the one object, as we have seen, that he does not want and will not have! That is his dilemma. That is his predicament. And that is his sin.

Here, then, is the answer to the sneers of the sceptics. Before a man will turn to Christ something is needed beyond a great capacity to believe. Some *supernatural answer* must be found. Something must take place to change the man's heart. His hatred of God must be destroyed. As he is, the natural man may have great wishes, but they do not include a wish to love and serve God. Nothing could be further from his mind. He will die rather than trust and follow his Enemy.

The supernatural answer is the new birth, regeneration. If the Bible provides the facts about Christ, the new birth provides the inclination to receive those facts and to rely on Him. You will remember these words from the last chapter about Michael and Mary:

'And if I must know . . . why Michael trusts Mary, it will come down to this. In his eyes she is trustworthy. He thinks he sees the evidence that it is so . . . And not only that, he wants her. His desire, his inclination is towards Mary. Both ingredients are there: trustworthiness (as he sees it), and inclination. Where these two meet, there we have the answer to the question, "How do we come to faith in a person?" '

The process is the same in trusting Christ. But the man must be different. Any *old man* can trust Mary or Michael or Harry or you or me. But only a *new man* can trust Christ.

In the right circumstances Mary and Michael and Harry and you and I can seem trustworthy and desirable to those around us. But no change of circumstances can make Christ attractive to the natural man.

Only a new heart can do that. And a new heart must come from God.

In closing this chapter let me pose a question. Should a sinner wait until he has a new heart before he commits himself to Christ? Does he dare do anything other than to wait? If he cannot and will not turn to Christ without a new heart what else can he do but wait? If regeneration must come first what choice does he have? The answer seems obvious.

The obvious answer, however, is not the right one. Not in this case. And it is important for us to understand this. Let us see if I can make my meaning clear.

The question I have raised suggests that I can know whether I am regenerate, the possessor of a new heart, apart from faith in Christ. But that is false. Apart from repentance and faith I cannot feel or discover the new birth. There is no way to know that I have been born again except by my new attitudes towards God and Christ. Those new attitudes are repentance and faith. If I refuse to turn to Christ until after I feel the new birth I shall never turn.

The gospel does not tell me to feel the new birth and *then* to turn to Christ. It commands me to turn *now*! And it assures me that when I do so, I have given all the evidence that I can give that I have been born again. Any reluctance to commit myself to Christ is not praiseworthy. At best it is a misunderstanding. At worst it is rebellion.

If the sinner, burdened under the load of sin, is to find relief, how will he find it? By looking at himself? Not at all! Let him not at this stage ask the question, 'Have I been born again?' Let him not even ask

121

whether he feels his sin as strongly as he might and should. Such questions take his attention away from the Lord Jesus. Instead, let him turn from his sin and cast himself on Christ. The way of peace and safety is not found in ourselves. It is found in looking to Him!

11: *True Faith and False*

I said in the last chapter that there is no way to make Christ attractive to the natural man. All through the Bible that point is made. It is made and it is illustrated in the accounts of the way men treated Jesus. They mocked Him. They tormented Him. Finally, they killed Him. And we are made to understand that the hatred that lies behind murder was present in the masses of men, even in those who never laid a hand on Him. The hearts of all natural men were against Him.

When we see three thousand come to Christ at Pentecost we must not misunderstand what is happening. This is not a parade of natural men. Peter has no new formula for making Christ attractive. Could Peter, with words, paint a more appealing Christ than men could see when Christ walked among them? Surely not. The thought is not only ridiculous, it is repulsive.

How, then, do we explain Pentecost? Not by reference to man, but by reference to God. We are meant to see that God is behind those conversions. Peter did not succeed where Christ apparently failed. Both Christ and Peter 'succeeded' or 'failed' just to the extent that God gave men new hearts – no more, no less. (Of course, real success for the minister of the gospel is not found in results but in faithfulness to his task. Christ, of course, was perfectly successful.) Those who came to Christ at Pentecost were no longer natural men. God changed them, and hence they believed.

Nevertheless, some in the New Testament are said to believe in Christ, who do not have new hearts. Who are they? They are men with a false faith. And they are put there, I do not doubt, for our instruction. If we want to know what faith is, we may learn by seeing what it is not. If we heed Jesus when He talks of false faith, we will more nearly catch His meaning when He speaks of faith that is true.

Listen to Jesus on the familiar parable of the sower. Since He interprets this parable I will put His story and His interpretation in parallel columns:

Behold, a sower went forth to sow; and when he sowed, some seeds . . . fell upon stony places, where they had not much earth: and forthwith they sprung up, because they had no deepness of earth: and when the sun was up, they were scorched; and because they had no root, they withered away.

He that received the seed into stony places, the same is he that heareth the word, and anon with joy receiveth it; yet hath he not root in himself, but dureth for a while: for when tribulation or persecution ariseth because of the word, by and by he is offended.

And some fell among thorns; and the thorns sprung up and choked them. (Matthew 13:3-7)

He also that receiveth seed among the thorns is he that heareth the word; and the cares of this world, and the deceitfulness of riches, choke the word, and he becometh unfruitful. (vv. 20-22)

(I have left out the parts of the parable that are not about false faith.)

In this parable Jesus is telling us how different kinds of people act when they hear God's word. He cites four classes of men. First, some hardly notice the word. And last, some believe and obey it. In between are those who say they receive it but later fall away. I have quoted their stories above. They are the false believers.

Why do I call them false believers? Why not call them temporary believers instead? Two preliminary points will help clear this up. First, Jesus shows us that the soils represent the hearts of men (v. 19). The soils vary as hearts vary. Second, it is plain that the condition of each of the soils *at the outset* determines the outcome. There is no question of soil that is bad becoming good, or *vice versa*. When the seed reaches the soil we can tell from Jesus' description how things will turn out. Good soil will bring forth fruit and bad soil will not.

If Jesus had meant us to think of some of these men merely as temporary believers He would have spoken differently (of course, their profession *was* temporary. They endured 'for a while'). Jesus would have shown us good soil becoming bad soil. In His interpretation we could have seen good hearts going bad. But that is not what He shows us. No, the stony soil was stony from the beginning. And the thorny ground was always thorny in the story. So 'false believers' is a better phrase than 'temporary believers' for these men.

It seems to me that there are but two ways for a professed faith to be false. Let us for a moment call faith 'trust in Christ'. Here we have two main parts. First there is trust. Second there is Christ. If faith is to

125

be false it will have to be false in one or the other. It will have to be something less than *trust*, or it will have to fix itself on something other than *Christ*. Each, I think, is illustrated in this parable.

Let us look at the stony-ground hearer. What was his problem? He certainly did not despise the word. Jesus tells us that he received it with joy. That was a promising sign. So far, so good! We are meant to understand that he professed faith in what he heard. He 'trusted in Christ'.

But the stony-ground hearer did not last. Why not? Jesus points out two things about him. First, he did not have root in himself. Second, he fell away when tribulation and persecution came. His not having root tells us that all was not well with this fellow's faith from the beginning. His falling away under persecution will help us to see what the problem was.

Let me give our stony-ground hearer a name and put him in a 20th-century setting. That should help us to see him better. His name is Mark Johnson and he lives in Chicago. Mark, like most Americans, feels that something is missing in his life. He cannot quite put his finger on it. He has a good job as a department store manager. His wife, Nancy, is congenial and his children are reasonably well-mannered. Mark has no quarrel with his neighbours, not even with the crabby man next door.

Yet Mark would hesitate to say that he is happy.

One night while switching from one TV channel to another Mark comes across a television evangelist. Something in the preacher's manner attracts him. He sits back to hear what is said. First he is intrigued; then he is engrossed. 'Come to Christ,' Mark is told, 'and you will find peace and happiness.' Peace and happiness! Was this the whole message, or did Mark simply focus in to this one part?

It makes no practical difference. At the end of the broadcast Mark follows the evangelist in a prayer. 'Lord,' he prays, 'I turn from my sins and take you as my Saviour. Come into my life and take over. I trust you, Jesus, with all my heart. Amen.' And Mark means every word of it.

Now I do not mean to take issue either with the evangelist's message or his method. I have my own thoughts about them, of course, but my thoughts are irrelevant just now. I say that for this reason: the greatest evangelist of all, the Lord Jesus, had stony-ground hearers. No doubt some messages and methods are more apt than others to call forth false faith. But that is not the point here. No matter how careful the evangelist is, the Mark Johnsons of this world will be led astray. For, like the rest of us, they see what they want to see and hear what they want to hear. And they are sincere in doing so.

Mark Johnson is apt to prove to be a stony-ground hearer, the kind who fixes his faith on something less than Christ. His prayer was, 'I trust you, Jesus, with all my heart.' Nothing wrong with that prayer! And no doubt he meant what he prayed. But who is this *Jesus* to whom Mark spoke? Is He the Lord Jesus Christ of Scripture? Or is he the product of Mark's imagination? Is He Lord of all? Or is he merely the supplier of peace and happiness? To put it another way, Is Mark now His servant, or is He the servant of Mark? It may seem cruel to ask questions of this kind, but we cannot do without them. These are the questions we must ask if we want to sort out true and false faith.

127

The Lord Jesus often faced this problem with His hearers. When He preached He taught men who already had an idea of what the Messiah, the Christ, would be like. They brought that idea with them when they came to hear Jesus. Their notion was largely political. The Messiah, as they saw it, would get rid of the Romans. Oh how they hated Rome and longed for liberty! 'When Messiah comes,' they whispered to one another, 'he will drive out the Romans. Then we'll be free.' They could hardly wait.

How did such men, men ripe to deceive themselves, react to Jesus? As you might expect. They sought to make Him their king. And they meant it. They were ready to entrust themselves to Jesus the Messiah. They were dead serious about it. 'Let's get on with it,' they said. 'Now that we've found the Messiah, where do we sign up?'

Perhaps some said these things thoughtlessly, but others had counted the cost. The Roman legions were all around them to keep men from deluding themselves for long. To sign on with the Messiah of their dreams could cost them their lives. Yet many were ready to do it. Their trust was real. It was wholehearted. They were in earnest. No turning back!

But, of course, it was not the real Jesus that they trusted. Not the real Jesus? No, it was a political hero of their imagination that they committed themselves to. Long before, in fact, they had put themselves in this hero's hands and they had watched breathlessly till he came into sight. When they saw him in Jesus they were ready to follow him. Later, when they no longer saw him in Jesus, they washed their hands of Jesus and looked elsewhere.

But we must not call this fickleness. It was not that

at all. First and last they were faithful to their ideal. But their ideal was not Jesus of Nazareth. Their trust was genuine, but it was not in the Son of God.

The clue to the stony-ground hearer is the *unexpected*. Listen to Jesus again:

> He that received the seed into stony places, the same is he that heareth the word, and anon with joy receiveth it; yet hath he not root in himself, but dureth for a while: for when tribulation or persecution ariseth because of the word, by and by he is offended.

The unexpected is what makes him give up. 'I didn't count on this,' he says. And off he goes to fairer (or fouler) fields.

Now the unexpected takes many forms. To men who looked for a political saviour, preaching peace was the unexpected. Words like 'the meek shall inherit the earth' would first confuse and finally alienate such men. Blood, sweat, and tears were what they looked for. Jesus' talk about meekness was startling and sickening. They would turn back to the world. Enough of *this* Messiah, *this* Christ! Their trust was real enough. But it was not in the real Christ.

Their case, however, was exceptional. Those men would have welcomed tribulation. That is what they expected. Their arms were open to embrace it.

A far more common case is the opposite of theirs. It is the case of the man who 'comes to Christ' to satisfy his everyday needs. With him the unexpected takes a different form. Tribulation is the last thing he wants or expects. Peace and happiness are his goals. 'Serenity' is his word – give him that and he is content. No surprises, please!

But you cannot have Christ without surprises – not

129

the real Christ. Let me make it more pointed. You cannot have Christ without *unpleasant surprises*. That is the way it is. That is the way He wants it, and in this as in all else Christ gets His way. He is determined to confront you and me and every other Christian with the unexpected. And I mean the *unpleasant unexpected*. A man who cannot bear to have his apple cart over-turned can trust *a* christ, but he cannot trust *the* Christ. Such a man may have faith, but it will not be faith in the Son of God.

The stony-ground hearer, then, is the man with faith in something less than Christ. Tribulation or persecution or talk of meekness opens his eyes. When Christ tests his faith (as He tests all profession), this man realizes his mistake. He wanted something less than Christ. He heard of something less than Christ. He trusted something less than Christ. 'I didn't count on things turning out like this,' he says as he backs away from Jesus. 'This is not the person I believed in.' His faith was real enough, but it was not faith in the risen Lord. He had the right attitude (faith), but the wrong object (a Christ of his own making). For that reason his faith was false.

There is another kind of false faith. We see it in the thorny-ground hearer. Let me set his brief story before you once more, along with Jesus' interpretation.

And some fell among thorns; and the thorns sprung up and choked them (Matthew 13:7).

He also that received seed among the thorns is he that heareth the word; and the care of this world, and the deceitfulness of riches, choke the word, and he becometh unfruitful (v. 22).

In this man's case we do not ask whether he

understood who Christ was. We need not go as far as that. It is true that he too said, 'I trust in Christ.' But Jesus shows that he had no wholehearted commitment to Christ. All along it was Christ *and* —. Christ *and* riches; Christ *and* the world. The thorny-ground hearer is the very man Jesus had in mind when He said, 'You cannot serve God and mammon.' (Mammon means 'property' or 'riches'.)

And that raises some searching questions. Must my faith be perfect? How far may something or someone besides Christ share the heart of the believer? If I trust in Christ, may I have faith in no one else? Such questions seem to demand answers. Let us see what we may say about them.

First, let me say something quite safe. My faith and your faith are not yet perfect. They are not all they should be – or will be. God has not finished with us. We are enrolled in the school of faith. Perhaps I have reached the third grade and you are up to the seventh. There are still more lessons to be learned, however, and still more grades to attain. We are in for the whole course and it takes a lifetime. We are not yet home.

It will cheer us to remember how the Lord Jesus treated imperfect faith. In a great storm He answered the cry of those whom he called men 'of little faith'. Not only that, He warmly commended faith no larger than the tiny seed of a mustard plant. That means this: the thorny-ground hearer's problem lay elsewhere. It was not merely that his faith was imperfect. Something else was wrong with the thorny-ground hearer.

Second, I am glad to make one more confident claim. The heart that belongs to Christ is bigger than it was before. It is broader and higher. It has more room for others, not less. If my experience counts for anything, once you come to Christ you find lots more people to have faith in. The body of Christ is a big family, and you want to share your heart with all. In Christ it is a *duty* to love others and to take them into your heart. Jesus commands it. To do it rightly you may have to think a good deal about your money and your property. And while you do that you have the blessing of Christ.

Faith in Christ does not mean that you never fix your mind on anything else. A man who literally gives no thought to this world will soon die. If nothing else gets him, starvation will carry him off. The thorny-ground hearer's problem was not that he thought about this world and money. Not at all! He had to do that, or perish.

What, then, was the thorny-ground hearer's problem? Simply this. In his heart the world and riches were in competition with Christ. Christ loves company, but not competition. He is not like the selfish man who wants to keep the girl he loves from seeing and meeting any other men. There is room in the Christian heart for any number of men and ideas. But there is room for only one lord. That Lord is the Lord Jesus. The man who thinks that he can serve Christ and another lord is deceiving himself. And the deception is fatal.

The thorny-ground hearer, then, is the man with something less than *trust* in Jesus. Yes, he believes after a fashion. He accepts many facts concerning Christ as true. But he is not committed to Christ. His attitude is less than Biblical faith. For that reason his faith is false.

It is time to sum up. In the last section I found that I had to use the words 'commitment' and 'committed' to make my point. Now I want to tell you why I used those words and why I think they mean the same as 'faith'.

Earlier we saw that faith in a person is habitual reliance on what that person says. That definition, of course, applies to faith in anyone. But we are interested in applying it to Christ, and He is God in the flesh. What kind of difference will that make? Let us see.

One reason you trust the people whom you trust is this: they know their own limitation. If they do not, you do not trust them. If John, for example, who is a good fellow but knows nothing of your job, insists on telling you how to do it, what will happen? You will soon lose some of your faith in him. You will say, 'If John goes on this way about my job, when he doesn't know what he is talking about, I wonder what else he thinks he knows that just isn't so?' You will think this way unbidden. No one will need to prompt you.

We can go a step further. What if John intrudes his 'knowledge' into other areas of your life where he is ignorant? What then? The answer is easy. You will give up relying on John for almost everything. Why? Because John appears to be playing God. An all-knowing God you can believe in; an all-knowing John you cannot.

But with Jesus Christ things are different. The Bible calls us to 'habitual reliance' on 'God in the flesh'. In Christ we find all the wisdom and knowledge and power of God, and His word bids us believe that He is able to apply all these to our case.

Now you will see at once what this means. It means that if I habitually rely on Christ I must trust not only in His promises but in much else also. Why? Because He is like John in my illustration. He makes His way

133

into all of life – my life. As God He can do nothing else. I must, if He is God, trust His claims and His commands as well. If He says, as He does, that He is to be my Lord, I must trust Him in this matter. If He says, as He does, that I must love my neighbour, I must believe that infinite wisdom shaped that command. It is implied in that command, as in all His commands, that what He commands is the best thing for me to seek to do.

There is no way around this. If Christ makes a claim, it is true. If He gives a command, it arises from infinite knowledge and wisdom. If He makes a promise, there is infinite power to carry it out.

What then? Just this: I may say that I believe these things, yet go on my way and do as I please. But it is silly for me to say that I trust in Christ if I act that way. No, if I believe these things are true and if I trust in Christ, my trust is just 'commitment', no more and no less. I commit myself to Christ's care. In embracing Christ I have committed myself to Him.

There are many men whom I rely upon, whom I have faith in. These men know their limitations. They accept them and I accept them, and we get on quite well. But in Jesus Christ I meet another sort of Man. He is the God-Man. He accepts no limitations on Himself. I must accept none. To believe in Christ, to trust in Him, to rely upon Him is just to give myself up to Him to take His orders as well as His comforts. Faith like that is *commitment*. I do not believe in Christ if I have not committed myself to Him. If I have committed myself to Him I have faith. The two things are parallel.

At the very outset of his Christian life the Christian committed himself to Christ. The stony-ground hearer committed himself to something less than the Christ of the Bible. The thorny-ground hearer apparently divided up his commitment. Later, though, it was shown that he was committed to mammon. But if we are true believers, we committed ourselves to Christ.

Look at the words again: *we committed ourselves to Christ*. That does not mean that our commitment was perfect. Nor could we see all that 'commitment' implied. Mercifully, much was hidden from us. The *unpleasant surprises* of which I spoke earlier have often set us back.

At no time could our timid commitment save us. Only the One we were committed to could do that. Our commitment was not perfect, but it was real. The setbacks have not been our undoing. God has put our feet back on His path. At this late date – it has been many years for some of us – we are still on the way. Even the setbacks have helped us. We are more conscious than ever of our dependence on Christ. And, what is most important, we are beginning – just beginning, I fear – to like it that way.

12: *Why such a Gift?*

In this chapter I want to take up one question that lies behind all we have learned so far, The question is this. Why did God do things the way He did? Why did He make faith a gift?

The first thing to say is this: in this case, as in all else God does, we cannot know all of His reasons. We can, of course, know what He has revealed in His word. For the rest we may only bow our heads in submission and wonder. That is proper for us as His creatures. 'Why?' can be a very impertinent question. It often conceals (or reveals!) our impatience with God, as though we were better fitted to run things than He is. So we want to ask the question 'Why?' carefully. Always!

But what has God revealed? We have already seen the most obvious thing. There would be no faith in God at all if He left natural men to themselves. If God wanted men to have faith, that was reason enough to give it to them. That much is clear. It does not, however, seem to get us far. After all, as far as we can tell, God might have made men differently. Or, He might have kept men from falling into sin. He did not choose to do so. Why not? Does the Scripture throw some light on this question? It pleased Him – that's all I dare say. I cannot say more.

Given men as they are, however, we can go a step

136

further. We can say this: God has made faith a gift so that (1) He will get credit for our salvation and (2) we will not get the credit. I have chopped that last sentence up, and put numbers in it, deliberately. The answer has two parts. The first part corresponds to something in God; the second part, to something in us. I want us to look at both.

What is it *in God* that prompted Him to make faith a gift? I think I can see the answer in His word. It is His grace. God's grace is His attitude of kindness towards unworthy creatures. And what better way to show the height and breadth and depth of His kindness than to show it to men who spurned Him? So that is what God decided to do. And He has done it – lavishly! In Paul's words, God has

> quickened us together with Christ . . . that in the ages to come he might shew the exceeding riches of his grace in his kindness toward us through Christ Jesus. (Ephesians 2:5, 7)

The phrase, 'trophies of His grace', has perhaps been overworked. But it says what needs to be said. In eternity we shall look at ourselves and say, 'Here is the evidence that God is gracious – He has saved me!' We shall be the trophies in God's trophy case. Angels will peer at us and shake their heads in wonder at the 'exceeding riches of his grace'. This facet of God's character will be displayed, a facet that could be seen in no other way. Men and angels will be moved to worship our gracious God.

But here comes a problem. It is this. Is God's kindness really *kindness*, if what God seeks is for men to give Him credit? Is it really *grace* if what God wants

137

is men's worship? How do things stand in this case? Is there an easy answer to this question?

Yes, there is an easy answer. We may say that God is not concerned about Himself, but only about us. Our happiness and our success: these are the things that move God. See how easy that answer is! But it has this against it: it is utterly false!

Why is it false? Let us see.

The easy answer is false for two reasons. The first is this: there is no law that limits God to one reason for the things that He does. In fact, since He is God, He may have a myriad of reasons for each thing that He does. How simple we would like things to be! Then we could master it all! But even quite ordinary people like ourselves are not so simple. When I am asked why I did such-and-such a thing, how do I answer? Frequently I give my reasons, one—, two—, three—. Yes, one of them may be most important, but they are all true. Just think of the number of reasons I might have, *if I were God*.

What is the second reason the easy answer is false? It is this: God has told us that in all that affects us He has at least two things in view. They are, (1) His own glory and (2) the good of His people. These two motives lie behind all Christian experience. Does some joy come to us? It is for our good *and* for the glory of God. Does some sorrow overtake us? It is for His glory *and* for our good. Never mind that we cannot understand how it can be so. It is true. 'He that glorieth, let him glory in the Lord' (1 Corinthians 1:31), while he remembers that 'all things work together for good to them that love God' (Romans 8:28).

So then, as Christians, we believe God. When He speaks of 'the exceeding riches of His grace' we take

138

Him at His word. Grace – the attitude of kindness towards unworthy creatures – is part of the heart of God. It moves Him to save His people. It moves *them*, in turn, to give Him the glory for their salvation.

What is it in God that caused Him to make faith a gift? It is His grace. That much is clear. But now we come to the other side of the question, the part that denies any credit to us. What is it *in us* that caused God to make faith a gift? We must take that up next.

And here there can be little doubt about the answer. It is found in Paul's negative expression, 'lest any man should boast!'

Men are boasters, Paul says, but God means to cut off all occasion for boasting.

> For by grace are ye saved through faith; and that not of yourselves: it is the gift of God: not of works, *lest any man should boast*. (Ephesians 2:8, 9)

In these two verses Paul teaches us a great truth. It is this. God has saved men in a way that leaves them nothing to boast of. Or – to borrow another word from Paul – 'Where is boasting then? It is excluded' (Romans 3:27). As Martyn Lloyd-Jones once wrote, 'It is put out through the door and the door locked on it; there is no room for it here at all.' The way of faith excludes boasting; the way of works does not.

Of course, if we forget that faith is a gift we may still find a way to boast. If we think of faith as a 'decision' that is wholly up to us then there will be room for boasting in that. Let me illustrate what I mean.

Imagine with me a dating couple, Henry and Louise. One day Henry, as nice a young man as you will ever meet, says to Louise, 'Louise, I want to marry you. I want you as my wife. Will you marry me?' Now Henry has committed himself. Now the deciding whether there will be wedding bells is entirely in Louise's hands. What will it be – yes or no?

Louise, an observant young lady, is well aware of Henry's sterling qualities. So she says, 'Yes!' And they live happily ever after.

But one day a question pops into Louise's mind. 'Who gets the credit for my happiness?' When she thinks about *that* she says, 'Henry – of course!' And she beams at Henry in her imagination.

Louise, however, has not done reflecting. Another thought steals across her mind. 'It's true,' she says, 'that I had sense enough to see Henry as he really is. That's more than Bonnie and Edith could do!' And who are Bonnie and Edith? They are the two girls that cared nothing for Henry at all.

Now let's ask Louise's question once more. Who gets the credit for Louise's happiness? Henry, of course. But we are not done, are we? No! Louise gets some credit also. Yes, there may have been some of what the world likes to call 'luck' involved, but there is something beyond that. Beyond that a good deal of credit must go to any girl who is shrewd enough to know what a young man is like *before she marries him*.

You will see, I think, how this applies to our salvation. God has committed Himself as Henry did. Christ has said, 'Come unto me . . .' Now it is up to us, will we come or will we not? It looks like the wise (not to say *shrewd*) thing to do. So we come to Christ. And who gets the credit for our happiness? Christ, of course.

But we are not yet done, are we? No! We too get some credit. Not much, to be sure. But *some*! Just as

Louise sized up Henry and saw what Bonnie and Edith could not see, just so we saw Christ for what He was. And *that* was more than Joe and Jim and Jack and Martha and Margaret and Matilda did – or so it would seem!

I think I can make this even plainer. Look ahead to eternity. Note how dramatically different the lot of the believer and the unbeliever is then. A complete change from this world! In eternity, seeing the contrast, we would have constant reason to congratulate ourselves on our decision, *if it was really ours*.

In eternity, we shall be really and completely humble. That might lead someone to say, 'In eternity we won't want any credit for ourselves.' But is that so? It depends on what humility is. Is humility pretending that one has not been wise or good or intelligent? Not at all! Humility includes having a proper view of oneself. The Lord Jesus was humble, was He not? We can agree on that. Yet we cannot think of Him pretending that He was not wise or good or intelligent, can we? Surely not. His humility included this: He knew Himself. He knew what He was and He knew what He could do.

And that is the way we shall be in eternity. We shall know ourselves. We shall accept the credit for anything we have done. If our eternal bliss rests on our wisdom in deciding for Christ we shall accept the credit and congratulate ourselves for ever. In doing so we shall be humble, *if the decision was really ours*.

But, someone may say, 'Don't forget that accepting credit for something and boasting about it are not the same thing.' What shall we say then? Well, the man who says that is right. But the point to note is this: they both have the same starting point, something

141

good that I have done. They both have the same ground. They are not utterly different. One is an exaggeration of the other – the difference between, 'I accept credit', and 'I ACCEPT CREDIT!' And what God has done is to take the ground out from under us. Boasting is not only discouraged – it is excluded.

Let me illustrate. I recall a summer day in my early teens. I was working on an Ohio farm during hay harvest. Another young fellow and I were on a hillside. Though I was young, Jimmy was younger, so I was driving the team of horses. With monotonous regularity we would pitch some hay on to the wagon, move a bit further forward, and do the same thing again. One moment we were up on the wagon, tramping down the hay; the next we were down again pitching away. The only variation in our routine came when, every once in a while, Jimmy would say, 'Let me drive the team!' Since for boys of our age driving the team was reckoned a prestige job I was not inclined to let Jimmy do it!

Then, suddenly, I handed Jimmy the reins.

Please do not misunderstand me. There was nothing kind in what I did, nothing generous. Far from that! Instead I was reacting to fear, the fear that we had piled the hay too high, the fear that the wagon, being on a hillside, was about to turn over!

Jimmy eagerly grabbed the reins without guessing what was in my mind. I edged towards the side of the wagon to prepare to jump. Then, without further warning, over it went! I did not make the leap I planned. I simply fell. I had intended to push off of that hay, but in an instant and before I could do so the hay was gone. There was nothing to push against but thin air. And I dropped in a heap.

Doesn't that wagon picture what God has done with

the Christian? Instead of leaving the ground under us so that we could make a small leap on our own He has taken it away completely. Once the wagon had started over, all my options were gone. It was no longer a great leap versus a small one. Without a platform to push off of there could be no jump at all. In the same way God has kept us from shouting, 'I ACCEPT THE CREDIT!' by taking away even our right to whisper it. He has barred us from the exaggeration by removing our platform, by not allowing us any credit at all. Once again, boasting is not simply discouraged. It is excluded!

And now we must ask ourselves a question. What must I do, what must you do, to enter into the spirit of what God has done? How shall we react? What shall we say?

The surprising answer is: we must boast! The Christian is allowed to boast. More than that he is encouraged to do so, but on an entirely different ground. No shrewdness or wisdom or power or understanding of his own enters into the Biblical kind of boast. He has riches from God and Christ. Let him boast of them,

of Christ's cross (Galatians 6:14)
of Christ's creative power (Galatians 6:15)
of God's grace (Ephesians 2:8, 9)

Whenever and wherever the urge to boast comes on him let him remember Paul's words, 'He that glorieth, let him glory in the Lord!' (1 Corinthians 1:31).

13: *The Two Roads*

I think I see you, Christian, standing before two old paths. One is called 'the High Road'; the other, 'the Low Road'. A weather-beaten gate opens into each. On the gate to the High Road a hand has chiselled the word 'WHO'. On the gate to the Low Road that same hand has carved 'WHY'. You are about to enter one of these paths. But which shall it be? In this case the decision is yours.

The path behind the gate marked 'WHY' is a jagged path. Many a pilgrim has been seen bleeding and disheartened in this road. It is easy to stumble on the Low Road. I'm sorry to say that more than one pilgrim has insisted on following this path all his life.

The path behind the gate marked 'WHO' is a friendlier path. Not so many pilgrims start out on this road, but all along the way a man may catch a glimpse of a brother or sister climbing upwards seeking to find a route from the Low Road below. Times without number I have seen a pilgrim on the High Road reach down a hand to someone below and tug at him till he is up and over the edge. It is a great sight to see.

The Low Road marked 'WHY' is the path of the Christian who insists on knowing the reason for all that happens to him. He needs to know in specific detail. He is not satisfied with the general answer: it is for your good and the glory of God. He needs more. He insists on more.

The man on the Low Road is bound to be disappointed. We have but one revelation from God – the Bible – designed to answer our detailed questions. Yet the Bible does not tell us in detail why *all* things happen to us. Take the experiences of just one day. How many things will happen to us today? Ten? One hundred? One thousand? I know no way to count them. But if I cannot count them how shall I analyse them all? How shall I find the reasons for them? I cannot.

Yet some men will select the more important events of their daily lives and brood over them. 'There must be a reason for this,' they say. 'Why did God allow this? Why did He send it my way?' And they feel that either (1) God owes them an answer, or (2) He has given it and they are too dense or unspiritual to see it. Either conclusion is disheartening.

The whole process is complicated in another way. Occasionally, but not often, God gives us a glimpse of what He is doing. I think, for instance, of the story we hear now and then of a Christian missing an air flight that later crashes. He reasons rightly that God was not finished with him. That much of God's intent could not be missed. But most of life is not like that, and 'why?' crops up to haunt us again and again.

Men do not give up thinking when they enter the High Road. 'Why?' can be a useful question. It is heard on the High Road as well as on the Low. But the difference is this. On the High Road a Christian is able to relieve his anxiety. When he can find no reason *why*, he is content to go a step further. The High Road is

145

the road where they concentrate on 'WHO', that is, on God.

In the earlier chapters of this book I shared with you an important truth. I said, in effect, that God was the author of salvation from beginning to end. Each man who is saved comes to Christ because God chooses to save him.

By saving whom He pleases God gets the glory and men are kept from boasting. Those are two good Biblical explanations of our salvation at the hand of God.

But no one supposes that those reasons tell the whole story. At least I do not. Perhaps, in our present condition, they are all that we can grasp. I believe it was Martin Luther who once made a helpful distinction. He divided the Christian man's life into three periods: nature, grace, and glory. Then he said in effect, 'Grace has revealed a good deal that nature did not. Can we not also believe that glory will reveal what grace has not?' Yes, we can believe that, for 'now we see through a glass, darkly; but then face to face' (1 Corinthians 13:12). Or in the words of an American gospel song, 'We will understand it better by and by.'

But something more must be said. If there is more to know and we can not know it now, that also is no accident. God could have made us differently originally. Or, He could give us greater capacity for understanding now. If God has not done these things, *that* too is a telling fact. That also needs explaining, and a cursory reading of the Bible will, I think, suggest the answer.

The Bible reveals God. The Bible reveals who God is. It unveils His works over many centuries. Yes, the purpose of the Book is to bring us to know God. In the words of Christ: 'This is life eternal, that they might know thee the only true God' (John 17:3). Let me say it again: *the purpose of the Bible is to bring us to know the character of God*. To put it another way, the Bible is not an end in itself, it is a means to an end, and that end is the knowledge of God. Those who take the High Road have learned this. When they are exhausted from wrestling with WHY they fall back on WHO. They fall back on their knowledge of God.

The fact that God gives faith to some and not to others raises questions about the justice of God. They are questions that I cannot answer. I am tempted here to write down my half-answers for you, for I think I have made some progress, but I will not yield to the temptation. Half-answers, for the man who has not worked them out for himself, are no answers at all. And half-answers do not satisfy even the man who has them.

So, what can I do? I'll tell you what I have done, and what I think you must do. I have fallen back on the character of God.

God is just. That means that He will never plan an injustice – not to any man, not to the wickedest sinner who ever lived. *God is also wise*. That means that He knows how to carry out His just plans. There is no question of His not knowing what injustice is. *God is all-powerful too*. He never lacks the resources to put His justice into effect. The answer to our difficulties, you see, lies in a knowledge of God.

And God has designed things that way. That is the reason we know no more than we do. It is not our lack of spirituality or our denseness when compared to other Christians. In fact, the more 'spiritual' Christians – whoever they may be – have the same intellectual problems that we have. God has made things that way. And, of course, He made them that way because He wanted to. And there we must leave the problem.

But all this raises another question: what precisely *is* the knowledge of God? What is it that I fall back on when I fall back on the knowledge of God? I raise this question because we use the word 'know' in two distinct ways when we speak of knowing a person. First, we say we know someone when we have been personally introduced to him, when we have shaken his hand and chatted with him for a few minutes perhaps. In other words, when personal contact has been made.

Second, we use the word 'know' when we have gathered information about someone. We may say, 'I know Napoleon well. I have studied his life for thirty years.' In this second use we are not claiming personal contact. But we are talking about a real knowledge of Napoleon.

Now, when we speak of the knowledge of God we mean both these things. We mean that we have had personal contact with God. We also mean that we have gathered facts about Him. Each is important. They are, however, important in different ways. Let me see if I can make this clear.

Personal contact with God does not supply us with information. Instead, it gives us a new attitude, a new state of mind. We receive the disposition to take in and apply the truths God has given us in His word. The new birth, for instance, is a touch from God. It is personal contact. The result of the new birth is the disposition to trust God. But it is the Bible that tells us in detail the character of the God we trust. The personal touch that we call the new birth does not do that.

The same is true of every touch from God. We all enjoy the feeling of nearness to God. There are times in Christian experience when we may say with Jacob, 'Surely the LORD is in this place!' May it please the Lord to grant us more such times! But there is danger here. There is the danger of focusing on the feeling of nearness and neglecting the *truth*.

I fear that many Christians have fallen into this trap. It is not that they do not read the Scriptures. It is rather that they do not read them *for information*. In fact, they sometimes harbour a suspicion that it is not quite spiritual to read the Bible for the truth it contains. The Bible, they think, must be read *devotionally*. But ask them what that means and they cannot tell you. Still they know it is true: the Bible must be read in a devotional way.

What shall we say in reply? The thing we need to say is this: they are right, of course, in what they say. But they must seek to understand what devotional reading is. Devotional reading is the opposite of academic reading. We can contrast reading *devotionally* with reading *academically*. But first let us compare them. What do they have in common? They have this in common: both types of reading are done for information. The devotional reader reads for information. The academic reader reads for information. Keep this in mind; the difference does not lie here.

What is the difference then? We may see it by looking more closely at that word *devotional*. The devotional reader is *devoted to* what he reads. That is, he feels loyalty to it. He is committed to it. He is faithful to it, or at least that is his intention. He may fall woefully short, but he aims to be true to what he reads.

149

The academic reader, on the other hand, is not committed to what he reads. He is reading for information *alone*. He may some day be committed to what he is now reading, but at this time he is not.

No Christian can be a merely academic reader of the Bible. A Christian is committed to the Scriptures. But a Christian *can* fall short of reading the Bible devotionally without realizing it. He may seek to read the Bible *emotionally*. Let me explain what I mean.

The academic reader is not usually greatly moved by what he reads. But the devotional reader is. Facts *that concern us* are deeply moving. When a man becomes a Christian he is deeply stirred by facts. He may have known these facts for some time, but now he sees their bearing on himself. That makes the difference. They come home to him. He may become ecstatic over truths that meant nothing a week before. His emotions come to life. Often Christian experience starts out like that.

Now comes the pitfall. Unless the new believer has never before been exposed to Christianity he is likely to underestimate the important part that *learning truths* has played in his conversion. Suppose he has grown up in a Christian home. He hardly remembers when he learned these truths. He has known the facts concerning Christ since childhood. Now, at last, he has embraced Christ. His life is transformed. He sees the world with new eyes. He hears music he has never heard before. All things are new. Is it any wonder if he gives more thought to his experience than he does to the truths which made it possible? And the more dramatic the experience the greater the risk would seem to be.

Let us say that he is now told that he must read the

Bible devotionally. What does this mean? It is likely to seem to mean that he must read in such a way as to prop up his new-found *feelings*. Keep your spiritual temperature up – that's the idea! And what about this advice? The advice to read devotionally is sound as far as it goes. But it does not go far enough. The man newly born again needs to be told what that means. He needs to be told that the impression that has been made on him has been made by *truth*. To be more exact, by *truths*, the truths concerning himself and the Lord Jesus. He is to read, then, in a certain way. He is to seek out God's truths and to give his loyalty to them.

I fear that many Christians read with the idea of inducing that same emotional state again. The Bible may come to be seen as a book that creates a kind of spiritual atmosphere. It may be seen as a mystical book. If one reads a set amount each day he is more likely to have this 'influence' go with him through the day. Never mind that he does not recall what he has read. At least he has had his 'devotions'. That is the best way to shore up his feelings through the day.

But it will not work. Why? Because God did not plan the Bible to work on our emotions directly. God did not intend to produce an aura of good feelings around the Bible reader. He intended, rather, to supply information. He aimed at teaching truth.

Has it ever struck you how lightly the Bible touches some matters? Take the crucifixion of Christ. Or, take the reality of hell. Notice how chastely it treats them. There is no effort to wring emotion from us. We see and feel the writers' restraint. We are not served up an atmosphere heavy with excitement. The facts are allowed to speak for themselves. The Bible is not an emotional book *in that way*.

If we are given the facts and if we are devoted to them – committed to them – our feelings will take care of themselves. If we read the Bible in this frame of mind we are reading devotionally, regardless of how we feel. To retain our emotional highs is not necessary. To keep up our commitment is.

And that brings us back to the knowledge of God. What do we fall back on when we fall back on the knowledge of God? We do not fall back on some recaptured 'devotional' feeling. We fall back on information. We review the truths about God's Person, His character, revealed in the Scriptures. Nothing more – what more could we want? And nothing less – nothing less will do. The High Road is the road where men concentrate on 'WHO'. They ask their questions. But when the answers escape them all is not lost. On the High Road pilgrims rest on the known character of their God. And, on the High Road, as on any other road, 'rest' feels good.

And now we are almost through. But before I close I want to speak to two questions that may have formed in your mind while reading this book. The first question is this: Do I really have faith? And the second is: How much faith must I have? These are good questions. And, judging by my experience, they are the kinds of questions that come up in the course of a study like this.

From one standpoint, both questions have the same answer. Not, of course, that anyone else can tell you whether you have faith in Jesus Christ. But help can be given, and I would like to give that help, if I can.

Mark this well: IT IS JESUS CHRIST WHO SAVES, AND NOT OUR FAITH.

What does that mean? It means that in talking about faith it is fatal to become mainly occupied with ourselves. We love to think about ourselves. And therein lies our danger. The man who would know whether He has trusted Christ needs to think on Christ.

The Bible compares the Christian life to marriage. In marriage a man and woman commit themselves to one another. The commitment of each is real. Yet neither the bride nor the bridegroom dwells on his or her own commitment. Rather, each thinks on the qualities of the other. Their commitment is drawn out by the qualities they see (or think they see) in the other.

And so it is with the Christian. The qualities he sees in Christ are the qualities of wisdom and nobility and truth. They are really there, and they draw the Christian. The creation of his faith, the strengthening of his faith, and the increase of his faith all come about from looking at the Lord Jesus. 'How much faith?' is the wrong question. The question is not 'how much faith?' but 'faith in Whom?'

Commit yourself to Jesus Christ. Do it immediately. Do it irrevocably. Think not of the size of your commitment, but of the greatness of Christ. Though it is true that God gives faith, it is also true that He does not sound a trumpet before Him and shout, 'I am about to give you faith!' Look at the Lord Jesus and see Him, trustworthy and glorious. If you can see Him in that way you will not find it hard to trust Him. And when you have committed yourself to the One who irresistibly draws you to Himself, you may be sure that it is the power of God that has done it.

You may be sure, in other words, that God has given you the gift of faith.

Beneath a dark first-century sky,
Condemned, our Saviour hung to die
Upon a Roman cross.
The mocking crowd pressed close to stare
Upon His broken body bare
Without a sense of loss.

Could anything in any age
Supply a surer, better gauge
Of mankind's moral plight?
Could any man expect to find
An ear so closed, an eye so blind,
As those before that sight?

But, yes, one ugly thing can vie
With every ear and every eye
Stopped up by hate that day,
My heart, before the light shone in,
Was just as deeply stained by sin
And bent beneath its sway.

Great God, has grace before this found
A mind so dull, a will so bound,
As it exposed in me?
Small wonder I shall love to sing
The mercies of my God and King
Throughout eternity!

Tom Wells
June, 1981

Appendix: *The Bible, The Word of God*

It is outside the scope of this book to defend the Bible as the word of God. It professes to be that, and nothing less, and I have treated it that way.

Occasionally, however, someone in the Christian community questions whether the Bible does indeed *profess* to be God's word. Just now, those theologians who have been called 'neo-orthodox' are raising such questions. This question is usually put forth by suggesting that later theologians have foisted this notion on the writers of Scripture. The writers themselves, we are told, would have never thought to identify their words with the word of God. The 'mechanical doctrine of verbal inspiration', we are assured, is the product of a much later age.

Now, whatever we may think of the doctrine of inspiration (mechanical or not!), one thing is clear. The fact that the Bible professes to be the word of God lies on the very surface of Scripture. This means that men or schools of thought that deny that fact are called on again and again to retract their denials. I cannot here trace the history of such turnabouts. To illustrate this kind of thing, however, I want to leave you with the following comments on two neo-orthodox theologians – Emil Brunner and Karl Barth – taken from Gordon Clark's *Karl Barth's Theological Method*, Presbyterian and Reformed Publishing Co., pp. 167–168:

... it may be remembered that Brunner in his earlier books asserted that verbal inspiration was a doctrine invented a century or so after the Reformation. Later he admitted that Calvin and Melanchthon held it, and then, even Luther. Retracting his earlier position he finally traced 'the false identification' of the Word of God with the words of the Bible to 2 Timothy 3:16 and even further back into the Old Testament. The doctrine of verbal inspiration therefore, divested of the pejorative adjective mechanical, is not an invention of the Renaissance ... Even Barth himself in another place [the reference is to Barth's *Church Dogmatics*, I. 1, p. 516] admits that verbal inspiration, far from being a Renaissance invention, was the teaching of Paul.

It must be understood that, though Brunner and Barth made these admissions, they were no more ready than before to simply identify the Scriptures with the word of God. They could not deny, however, that that is what the Scriptures profess to be.